South Africa's Post-Apartheid Foreign Policy – from Reconciliation to Revival?

Chris Alden and Garth le Pere

ADELPHI PAPER 362

Oxford University Press, Great Clarendon Street, Oxford OX2 6DP
Oxford New York

Athens Auckland Bangkok Bombay Calcutta Cape Town
Dar es Salaam Delhi Florence Hong Kong Istanbul Karachi
Kuala Lumpur Madras Madrid Melbourne Mexico City Nairobi
Paris Taipei Tokyo Toronto
and associated companies in Ibadan

Oxford is a trade mark of Oxford University Press

Published in the United States
by Oxford University Press Inc., New York

© The International Institute for Strategic Studies 2003

First published December 2003 by **Oxford University Press** for
The International Institute for Strategic Studies
Arundel House, 13–15 Arundel Street, Temple Place, London WC2R 3DX
www.iiss.org

Director John Chipman
Editor Tim Huxley
Design Manager Simon Nevitt

British Library Cataloguing in Publication Data
Data available

Library of Congress Cataloguing in Publication Data

ISBN 0-19-853078-1
ISSN 0567-932X

Contents

Glossary

ACCORD	The African Centre for the Constructive Resolution of Disputes
AISA	Africa Institute of South Africa
ANC	African National Congress
ASEAN	Association of South East Asian Nations
AU	African Union
CCR	Centre for Conflict Resolution
CHOGM	Commonwealth Heads of Government Meeting
DFA	Department of Foreign Affairs
DG	Director-General
DoD	Department of Defence
DRC	Democratic Republic of Congo
DTI	Department of Trade and Industry
EU	European Union
FRETILIN	Revolutionary Front for an Independent East Timor
GDP	Gross Domestic Product
GEAR	Growth, Employment and Redistribution strategy
HIPC	Highly Indebted Poor Countries
IMF	International Monetary Fund
IRPS	International Relations, Peace and Security
ISDSC	Inter-State Defence and Security Committee
ISS	Institute for Strategic Studies
MAP	Millennium Africa Programme
MDC	Movement for Democratic Change
MK	Umkhonto we Sizwe
MLC	Congolese Liberation Movement
MONUC	UN Observer Mission to the Congo
MPLA	Movimento Popular da Libertacao de Angola
NAI	New African Initiative
NAM	Non-aligned Movement

NCACC	National Conventional Arms Control Committee
NEPAD	New Partnership for Africa's Development
NPT	Non-proliferation Treaty
OAU	Organisation of African Unity
OECD	Organisation for Economic Cooperation and Development
OPDS	Organ for Politics, Defence and Security
PCAS	Policy Coordination and Advisory Services
RCD	Congolese Rally for Democracy
RDP	Reconstruction and Development Programme
SACU	Southern African Customs Union
SADC	Southern African Development Countries
SANDF	South African Defence Force
SPLA	Sudan People's Liberation Army
TBVC states	Transkei, Bophuthatswana, Venda and Ciskei
UNCTAD	United Nations Conference on Trade and Development
UNITA	National Union for the Total Independence of Angola
WTO	World Trade Organisation

Introduction

In 1994, South Africa emerged from decades of international isolation induced by its apartheid policies into a world in the grip of rapid and sometimes contradictory change. Fratricidal war in places as diverse as Bosnia, Sierra Leone and Sri Lanka had demonstrated the potency of communities of blood rooted in exclusion while globalising capital, spurred on by rapid advances in communications and technological innovation, had trampled borders in search of new consumers and markets.[1] The African continent, caught in a spiral of intermittent violence, rampant pandemics, economic decline and state collapse, appeared to be on the cusp of marginalisation from the promise of prosperity that accompanied the expansion of trade and diffusion of technology.

Against this backdrop, South Africans were challenged to construct new democratic institutions and an inclusive civic culture from the bitter legacy of decades of statutory racism and ideological division. Successive apartheid regimes had resorted to coercion and state violence to enforce what was universally condemned as illegitimate white minority rule.[2] The apartheid state embodied the instrumental architecture of domination and, with its security forces, sought to guarantee that dominance through the destabilisation of the southern African region. For the excluded majority, political life had no real meaning: it was without rights, citizenship and inclusive civil institutions, and consequently it turned to mass protest, trade union-activism and violent revolution.[3]

Given this bitter history, the plaudits hailing South Africa's negotiated political settlement and peaceful transition in 1994 were lyrical indeed. In the face of dour predictions of a racial war and harbingers of an apocalyptic future, its transition has been extolled as 'one of the most extraordinary political transformations of the twentieth century', in which South Africans 'have defied the logic of their past, and broken all the rules of social theory, to forge a powerful spirit of unity from a shattered nation'.[4] The most liberal of constitutions replaced the narrow hegemony of apartheid, and formed the cornerstone upon which the African National Congress (ANC) leadership attempted to universalise the state and its institutions in conjunction with civil society. New approaches were advanced, which stressed economic growth and redistribution, democratic institutions, individual liberties, human rights, rationality in public policy, inclusive norms and values and a common national identity.[5] At the same time, the evolution of an overarching national identity has contended with potent forces from the country's past.

Just as the fragile domestic situation presented a raft of challenges for the ANC, so the turbulent international environment – and especially its consequences in Africa – imposed specific and compelling demands upon the fledgling government in Pretoria. Building upon the legacy of the apartheid state and the liberation movement, the new South Africa sought to develop an activist role in international affairs. This was premised upon a belief in the compatibility of human rights, solidarity politics and the country's own development needs. From questions as diverse as Nigerian democracy to independence for East Timor, President Nelson Mandela and his successor Thabo Mbeki have sought to invigorate the conduct of international affairs with reference to South Africa's unique transition and moral stature. For the ANC, the struggle for an apartheid-free South Africa was in many ways a struggle for fundamental human rights. It was no coincidence, therefore, that human rights were canonised as a cornerstone of foreign policy.[6] There was a logical symmetry between the ethical and normative constructs of its domestic policies and the idealist foundations of its foreign policy.[7]

South Africa's seminal role in African affairs and, increasingly, as a vocal advocate on behalf of developing countries on the broader international stage, has ensured that it is seen as a key player in the emergent post-Cold War system. This is evident in a number of areas relating to both Africa and South Africa. In particular, South Africa has sought to play a key role in the resolution of a series of conflicts within southern and central Africa through active and sustained mediation. In pursuit of a comprehensive economic and political revival of the continent, South Africa has assumed a leadership position – in concert with other African partners – in the promulgation of new approaches and institutions in Africa, such as the economic blueprint of the New Partnership for Africa's Development (NEPAD) and the refashioning of the Organisation of African Unity (OAU) into the African Union (AU). Through its active participation in leading institutions of the South, such as the Non-Aligned Movement (NAM) and the UN Conference on Trade and Development (UNCTAD), South Africa has positioned itself as a bridge between North and South on vital questions of global governance, such as nuclear non-proliferation and Third World debt.

South Africa's dramatic rehabilitation from international pariah to bastion of African democracy is the product of a carefully crafted transition. Such is the hold of this arguably unique transformation that it continues to exert influence over the shape and conduct of foreign policy. This paper presents and analyses South African foreign policy from the onset of the democratic transition to the contemporary period. The focus is on the question of South African leadership in the context of this transition; the regional and continental challenges and opportunities it faces; and, more broadly, South Africa's aspirations to an international role in the South. It provides a comprehensive review of South African foreign policy over the past decade, including new material on key aspects of the transition and the consolidation of foreign policy under Mandela and Mbeki. It analyses critically the interplay between foreign-policy themes – human rights, development and security – at the regional and continental levels through an investigation of specific case studies in central and southern Africa. Finally, it investigates the role of South Africa in promoting an economic and political revival of the African continent, and its own part in reinvigorating the institutions of the South. In the course of the analysis of the South African case, this study seeks to answer the following questions:

- Will South Africa be bound (and able) to play the role of Africa's 'hegemon' and be a dominant partner on the continent through its superior economic, military and political presence, and what will the implications of such dominance be?
- What role have South African-led initiatives played, and will

continue to play, in resolving conflicts in southern and central Africa, and is South Africa able to assume the role of trusted interlocutor?

- How does post-apartheid South Africa reconcile a commitment to human rights with its trade, development and security imperatives?

- How does the nature of the transition within South Africa affect the formulation and implementation of post-apartheid foreign policy?

The paper shows how South Africa's ambitious foreign-policy agenda, the product of international expectations fostered in part by Mandela and the pan-African revivalism of Mbeki, needs to be tempered by an appreciation of the constraints that inhibit or circumscribe its ability to achieve these objectives. These limitations include:

- South Africa's pressing need for financial resources and foreign investment in regional peacekeeping or democratic-oriented advocacy;

- limited institutional capacity due to difficulties in the transformation of key foreign and security institutions, such as the Department of Foreign Affairs (DFA), the Department of Defence (DoD) and the South African National Defence Force (SANDF);

- continuing misapprehensions on the part of South African officials with regard to the complexity and content of Africa's international politics; and,

- persistent ambiguity over the nature of South Africa's identity, viewed from within a deeply divided society, and by African partners beyond its borders who remain sceptical of South Africa's aspirations to continental leadership.

Despite these limitations, it is the authors' contention that South Africa's post-apartheid foreign policy will continue to play a determining role in the security and development of the African continent, and in broader relations between North and South.

Chapter 1

Mandela and the Foreign Policy of Transition

On assuming power following the elections of April 1994, the ANC faced the formidable task of translating the gains of liberation diplomacy into a pragmatic and principled foreign policy. It also had to stamp its own philosophical imprimatur on foreign policy and refashion in its own image the institutional architecture inherited from successive apartheid regimes.

During Nationalist Party rule from 1948 to 1994, and particularly after 1976, South Africa was treated as a pariah state by the international community. The general opprobrium incurred because of apartheid policies and practices had a profound impact on the way South Africa was viewed internationally, and the manner in which it responded to external censure and sanctions. Apartheid governments adopted defensive, reactionary and combative strategies in order to offset the impact of isolation and punitive measures. According to a practitioner during the apartheid years, 'policy formulation was therefore limited to a handful of individuals who constituted a special kind of elite. For all practical purposes, Parliament played no role in foreign policy and the role of Cabinet tended to be limited to acquiescence or approval'.[1] Under President P. W. Botha's leadership from 1978–89, institutions such as the State Security Council were established as autonomous elements of the Foreign Ministry, countering what was perceived as a 'total onslaught' against the country.[2] This 'militarisation' of foreign policy meant that the full power of South Africa's armed forces was deployed in the region to contain an ostensible communist threat and to weed out

ANC guerrilla bases and training camps. The impact of political and economic sanctions was compounded by the ANC's policy of deepening South Africa's isolation by carrying to the world the UN declaration that 'apartheid was a crime against humanity'.

For the ANC, the struggle for an apartheid-free South Africa was a struggle for fundamental human rights. It was no coincidence, therefore, that once the ANC was in power, human rights became an important leitmotif in its foreign policy. In addition, the new government's approach was informed by a desire to make Africa – and southern Africa in particular – the primary theatre of South African activism, to promote regional development and to participate constructively in multilateral institutions. A broad approach of 'universality' was adopted, which represented the new government's intention to pursue a diplomacy of active internationalism. However, this new approach was bound by certain ideological inclinations and preferences inherited from its guerrilla past. The government as a result found itself in the invidious position of maintaining links with old friends and supporters of the ANC with dubious human-rights records, including the Indonesian New Order regime, the Nigerian military, Algeria, Libya and Cuba.[3] Attempts at reconciling the promotion of human rights with the practical concerns of restructuring the state occupied the bulk of Mandela's tenure in office. This task was further complicated by the unexpected complexities that accompanied the transformation of South Africa's foreign-affairs bureaucracy.

Constructing a new foreign policy

Mandela's declaration on the eve of the 1994 elections that 'human rights will be the light that guides our foreign policy' set the tone for the shape and conduct of South African diplomacy in the aftermath of apartheid.[4] By incorporating the experiences of the anti-apartheid struggle into the conduct of foreign policy, the ANC leader sought to imbue the practice of international affairs with an orientation towards the promotion of civil liberties and democratisation. Moreover, in keeping with the solidarity politics of the past, which had bound together liberation movements from East Timor to the Western Sahara, the new government maintained an openness towards the concerns of non-state actors, as well as a willingness to engage them.

Within this framework, special recognition was given to southern Africa, where South Africa had held economic sway for well over a century. South African involvement in the regional economy, whether as a provider or a recipient of migrant labour, transport services, hydropower or trade, has historically been significant both to South Africa and to other Southern African Development Community (SADC) countries.[5] Secondly, there was a strongly held belief that South Africa could not remain 'an island of prosperity in a sea of poverty', and that only through concerted regional development would some of the region's deep-seated problems (unfettered migration and undocumented trade, civil war and social disintegration, the traffic in illegal arms, contraband and drugs) be addressed.[6] Finally, the ANC and South African business community believed that greater involvement by South Africa in regional trade, sectoral cooperation projects and the joint development of regional resources and infrastructure could help to promote growth and development in both South Africa and the region.[7]

Active internationalism, primarily through multilateral institutions, was another feature of post-apartheid foreign policy. The government sought to reinvigorate these institutions with reference to South Africa's own unique political transition and the concomitant moral authority that came with unprecedented measures such as the unilateral dismantling of its nuclear programme. In particular, African-based institutions, such as the OAU, and organisations with a 'South' orientation, such as the NAM, were seen to be the proper setting for the promulgation of a reformist agenda that reflected South African interest in democratic practice and development.

These themes were outlined in a number of influential articles and documents produced by the ANC prior to the elections. Once in power, the government launched a consultative process which sought to engage civil society through a series of public meetings and the circulation of a discussion document. While the exercise elicited substantive responses from a range of actors, from independent foreign-policy think-tanks to anti-land mine campaigners, it never resulted in a government White Paper on foreign policy, as had been initially conceived. Despite this, it clearly played an important part in raising awareness of future directions for post-apartheid foreign policy, as well as beginning the slow process of legitimising the country's institutions for foreign policymaking.

Transforming the instruments of foreign policy

As in all other areas of public policy, the incoming government was confronted with the daunting challenge of reconstructing the institutions charged with foreign relations.[8] In its apartheid incarnation, the official business of the DFA had been directed almost exclusively at attempts to ward off international sanctions and diplomatic isolation. Unofficially, the DFA was involved in government sanctions-busting, military interventions in neighbouring countries and other activities that contravened international law.[9] With exceptions such as Malawi and Côte d'Ivoire, relations with the rest of Africa were uniformly hostile, and attention was focused above all on maintaining favour with Europe and the US. The 'independent homelands' of Transkei, Bophuthatswana, Venda and Ciskei (the TBVC states) had foreign-affairs departments and diplomatic representatives of their own, recognised only by South Africa.[10]

The DFA's role as the new custodian of foreign policy has been mired in controversy and disagreement within the Department. Achieving representative racial and gender balances has been a particular source of acrimony and tension since 1994. By 2000 while most of South Africa's career diplomats were black the total (non-politically appointed) staff complement of missions abroad remained skewed: 40% were black and 60% white. Moreover, the world views of the mandarins and practitioners representing the old and new orders were antithetical.[11] A common assessment was that South Africa's foreign policymakers are divided between 'internationalist' and 'neo-mercantilist' camps. Officials representing the previous government belonged to the latter group, which 'consistent with the logic of neo-realism, emphasise[s] the importance of trade and self-interest over all else'. The 'internationalists' were mainly those who returned from long years in exile with an orientation towards 'a demonstrably greater degree of solidarity with the collective problems of the developing world'.[12] The department was also perceived to suffer from a lack of assertive leadership, incapable of decisive policy and organisational transformation as well as managing the culture-clash between seasoned but suspect 'old order' bureaucrats and inspired but inexperienced liberation cadres.

On the basis of its history and evolution, the DFA emerges as a weak and ineffective bureaucratic player, lacking clarity of purpose and a long-term strategic perspective. Its internal divisions and inertia, together with competition from other actors, conspired (in most instances) to make it peripheral to the shaping and influencing of policy during the Mandela years. Although attempts were made to develop conceptual coherence, strategic direction and operational codes,[13] cleavages of race, gender, style and ideology persisted. While the skills and abilities of incoming ANC diplomats were generally high, with experienced personnel primarily deployed in the multilateral sector and occupying senior posts abroad, those with lesser abilities increasingly took refuge in patronage. The TBVC 'diplomats', whose retention in the civil service was part of the compromise struck during inter-party negotiations at the World Trade Centre outside Johannesburg, presented another dilemma for the foreign-policy bureaucracy as they were singularly ill-suited to their positions, but were protected by the new labour laws. The DFA therefore found itself suffering from important institutional shortcomings, including technical incompetence, a poverty of resources and the lack of a domestic constituency to act as an advocate of its concerns.[14]

In the process of exorcising nearly four decades of 'the diplomacy of isolation', the ANC seriously underestimated the scope and complexity of institutional restructuring and of managing the country's foreign policymaking machinery. South Africa's post-apartheid foreign policy soon fell victim to the perennial conundrum in foreign policymaking: the lack of a coordinated vision. Critics believed that South Africa's 'foreign relations could be said to be lacking the necessary broad orientation and strategic purpose'.[15] The main problem for South Africa's post-apartheid foreign relations was the emergence of multiple actors shaping, determining and implementing policy. This might not be surprising in an era of global financial markets, regional economic blocs, international trade linkages, and new forms of multilateral governance. While the DFA was the putative primary locus of expertise and implementation, it often found itself at odds with, if not in diametrical opposition to, a range of other actors – including the president, deputy president and various ministries – with claims upon the foreign-policy process. This multiplicity of actors encouraged accusations of incoherence, inconstancy and opaqueness in policy formulation.[16]

Meanwhile, the critical voices of civil society have merely added to the cacophony. This is understandable in view of the widening scope of international relations and the blurring of the traditional lines between domestic and foreign affairs – what has been called 'complex interdependence'[17] – where foreign policy now includes issues as diverse as investment, migration, energy, inflation, food security, human rights and the environment. Government leaders therefore 'find it increasingly difficult to set priorities, avoid contradictory targets, and maintain a sense of national interest and direction. Since the alternatives are more numerous and less clear-cut, the task of choosing becomes more complex'.[18]

Mandela's towering personality and international stature meant that he dominated every major foreign-policy decision, overshadowing the DFA, the cabinet and parliament. Mandela's international renown was such that 'it has meant South Africa's image (and its foreign policy) tends largely to be equated with the president's profile. As a result, policy has often followed his public statements, rather than the other way around'.[19] It is widely acknowledged that it was through his leadership that South Africa managed a successful and peaceful transition.[20] Although operating in his shadow, Thabo Mbeki, his deputy president and heir apparent, was the prime architect in reconfiguring South Africa's relations with the US, Europe, the South and Africa.[21] An experienced diplomat in his own right, during his long years in exile he emerged as the ANC's chief international spokesman and has retained his distinctly internationalist outlook.

Tensions and strained relations between the Department of Trade and Industry (DTI) and the DFA were acute. Since 1994, the DTI has emerged as the chief steward of South Africa's bilateral and multilateral trade diplomacy. Encouraging investment and foreign trade, in particular gaining preferential access to developed countries' markets, has become an important instrument in South Africa's economic development, export diversification and industrialisation strategy. The successes of the DTI in, for example, complex negotiations on a free-trade agreement with the European Union (EU) only fuelled personal as well as institutional antagonisms between the two departments. As security matters and arms sales have become an increasingly critical feature of South Africa's foreign relations, so the Department of Defence (DoD) has become a more prominent and contentious actor. It has often taken the lead on security-related matters, where the DFA has been relegated to a supporting role. Arms sales are regulated by a four-tier system, including the cabinet-level National Conventional Arms Control Committee. The DFA is partially responsible for providing the decision-making process with the necessary analysis and information, for instance on a recipient country's human-rights record, but the department has often been marginalised by the DoD's profit imperative and pressure to maintain the country's share of the global arms market.[22]

Parliament's primary role in foreign policymaking is to give the public an opportunity to express its views, and to act as a watchdog in the public interest. Despite having 266 members out of 400 in the National Assembly, ANC parliamentarians have often complained about their limited role in the substance of policy. Under Raymond Suttner, chair of the multiparty parliamentary portfolio committee on foreign affairs, parliament was active on selected issues such as diplomatic recognition for China and the arms trade, which at times came close to outright criticism of the government.[23] Nevertheless, a lack of resources and the pressure of party politics have consistently hampered the portfolio committee's oversight and review function.

South Africa's rich civil society includes a range of non-state actors concerned with influencing foreign policy, such as trade unions, civic organisations, human-rights groups and academic think-tanks. The sector has undergone a profound transformation since the onset of the democratic transition. The close alignment of civil society with the ANC's struggle for national liberation has given way to a sense of alienation and marginalisation as the government has usurped many of its traditional areas and co-opted many of its most talented members: 'many of the assumptions and affinities inherited from the anti-apartheid struggle have translated poorly into the new context. Disaffection with statist routes of transformation has coupled with the perception of the state "withered away" by globalisation, yielding hugely amplified assessments of the scale and role of civil society'.[24]

In 1994, there were great expectations that civil society would claim a special place for itself in helping to shape South Africa's foreign policy, especially the promotion of human rights and democratic values and norms. These hopes were raised by the ANC with its stated commitment to human rights and avowed aim to establish a policy discourse and formulation process that was open and participatory. The beginnings were auspicious. In June 1996, the DFA released its draft White Paper, the South African Foreign Policy Discussion Document. This invited a cross-section of academic and other civil-society interests to a forum where they influenced the prioritising of goals set out in the document. Most dramatically, non-governmental organisations helped to formulate South Africa's position in the international campaign to ban landmines as part of the so-called Ottawa process. They also made another significant contribution to the framework set out in the White Paper on South Africa's participation in peace missions. In the area of South Africa's multilateral diplomacy, civil-society representatives were important participants in developing the agendas for summits of the NAM, the UNCTAD and the Commonwealth. The complexities of South Africa's free-trade deal with the EU were made more manageable thanks to research and discussions with a range of NGOs. Several research organisations and NGOs were specifically asked to undertake analytical research and host conferences, workshops and discussion forums to help policymakers' thinking and strategies.

However, these collaborations masked areas of growing tension, particularly around the government's management of its human-rights diplomacy. Criticism of South Africa's 'liberation-era' links with regimes that abused and violated human rights were a particular source of tension, as were arms sales to such regimes. As South Africa appeared to jettison its human-rights emphasis in favour of a more pragmatic position, the voices of civil society became still more muffled. This was due in part to the great burdens placed on government officials. The need for decisions on difficult issues seemed to make consultation with civil society a luxury that could no longer be afforded.

Finally, a number of South African foreign-policy think-tanks were involved in 'second-track' diplomacy at the behest of the DFA. This was the case with the Foundation (now the Institute) for Global Dialogue, which was called upon to assist in the democratisation process in Nigeria through contacts with civil-society actors within the country, and exiled opponents of the regime. It was also involved in promoting dialogue with Lesotho's civil society in the aftermath of a South African-led incursion in 1998. The African Centre for the Constructive Resolution of Disputes (ACCORD) played a role in conflict management in the Congo and Sudan, while the Institute for Security Studies (ISS) was involved in disarmament, demobilisation and reintegration operations in Africa. The Centre for Conflict Resolution (CCR) became engaged in mediation efforts in Burundi in the mid-1990s, a measure that was later to pave the way for Mandela's own initiatives. Nonetheless, as the Mandela presidency drew to a close, civil society actors were increasingly frustrated in their efforts to influence South African foreign policy.[25] Their position has not improved under Mbeki.[26]

Problems of implementation

In the implementation of foreign policy, financial, commercial, political and defence interests supplanted the new government's carefully crafted ethical dimension. This reflected the government's adoption of 'an eclectic synthesis of neo-realist and neo-liberal principles, which remains cognisant of a globalising world economy'.[27] Rather than being guided by critical and principled perspectives, the inclination was to solve problems as they arose.[28] More often than not, this produced realist and pragmatic responses where a critical and principled position might have been more prudent. The following cases illustrate this policy dilemma.

The East Asian drama

In many ways, South Africa's relations with Indonesia best illustrate the contradiction between a commitment to human rights and the government's realist impulses. From 1994, South Africa and its president found themselves drawn into the long-standing conflict surrounding the status of East Timor in Indonesia. Mandela earned East Timorese gratitude for gaining President Suharto's permission to visit the imprisoned resistance leader Xanana Gusmao in July 1997, and for his call that autonomy be granted to the territory. However, he rapidly lost this sympathy during Suharto's visit to South Africa in November 1997, when he was given the Order of Good Hope, South Africa's highest honour for non-citizens.[29] Similarly, although Mandela wrote to Suharto urging him to release Gusmao and other East Timorese activists, the government expelled the Portuguese ambassador to South Africa after a copy of the letter was leaked to the South African press. During his July visit, Mandela had also controversially stated that South Africa would supply arms to Indonesia for external defence 'without hesitation'. South Africa abstained on resolutions criticising the Indonesian government's human-rights violations at the UN Commission on Human Rights in 1997 and 1998, and failed to condemn Indonesian security forces on the repeated occasions when gratuitous force was used during protests.

All of these actions came amid a rising tide of discontent among the ANC's alliance partners, the South African Communist Party and the Congress of South African Trade Unions. For these groups, ties of solidarity with Gusmao's movement, the Revolutionary Front for Independent East Timor (FRETILIN), and labour activists in Indonesia were deemed to be the appropriate point of departure for relations with Jakarta. Given Mandela's admission in 1995 that Indonesia had given 'generous financial assistance' to the cash-strapped ANC following visits to Jakarta before and after the 1994 elections,[30] even the ANC chairman of the parliamentary portfolio committee on foreign affairs was led to question the extent to which government policy was driven by the party's financial interests.

Similar questions have arisen around South Africa's relations with Malaysia, China and Taiwan, all of which are reputed to have made significant financial contributions to the ANC since it became the ruling party in government.[31] During his first official tour of Southeast Asia in March 1997, Mandela refused to abjure ties with countries that had poor human-rights records, stating that South Africa's foreign policy would not be 'influenced by the differences which exist between the internal policies of a particular country and ourselves ... There are countries where there are human rights violations, but these countries have been accepted by the United Nations, by the Commonwealth of Nations and by the Non-Aligned Movement. Why should we let ourselves depart from what international organisations are doing?'[32] Mandela did not question the decision of the Association of South East Asian Nations (ASEAN) to admit Burma as a member, nor did he use the opportunity to speak out on behalf of the detained pro-democracy leader and fellow Nobel Peace Prize laureate Aung San Suu Kyi.[33] General Khin Nyunt, 'Secretary-1' in the Burmese military regime, attended Mbeki's inauguration as president in June 1999.

On 28 November 1996, without warning, Mandela announced that South Africa would grant full diplomatic recognition to China and downgrade relations with Taiwan (established in 1976).[34] This ended the vexing 'Two China dilemma' which had preoccupied foreign-policy pundits and the government over the previous three years. In December 1997, DFA officials portrayed the South African government's decision as 'an opportunity to discuss with the Beijing government human rights issues at first hand'.[35] Yet at the same time, when asked whether South Africa had any concerns about China's human-rights record, Mandela stated that he preferred not to interfere in the domestic affairs of any country. In April 1998, Mbeki visited China and stated explicitly that he had not raised human-rights concerns during his trip.[36] When the Dalai Lama visited South Africa in December 1999 to attend a conference on world religions, Mbeki refused a private audience, fuelling speculation that he had bowed to pressure from China.[37] By April 2000, when Chinese President Jiang Zemin visited South Africa, official government statements focused on bilateral trade and commercial interests. Indeed, Pretoria and Beijing formed one of South Africa's closest relationships with a non-African country through active engagement in processes such as the China–Africa Ministerial Forum and substantive investment in each other's economies.

The Nigeria folly

Nigeria's political crisis in 1995 must rank as one of the most serious and potentially explosive challenges to confront the new South African government, testing the ANC's foreign-policy ideals and objectives in a very palpable and public way.[38] Because of Nigeria's support for the ANC in exile, many of South Africa's new leaders, including Mbeki, developed close links with the political and military elite there. Perhaps partly as a result, the new South African government adopted an ambivalent attitude towards the military regime in Nigeria: on the one hand, South Africa's own struggle led to a natural sympathy for the pro-democracy opposition; on the other, arguments about 'African solidarity' tended to support Nigeria against international criticism, especially from Western governments.

The immediate crisis began in 1993, when the head of the regime, General Ibrahim Babangida, annulled the results of elections which the opposition candidate Chief Moshood Abiola was widely believed to have won. Matters worsened considerably when Abiola was jailed for treason in June 1994 by General Sani Abacha, Babangida's more dictatorial successor. The new South African government found itself under pressure from various quarters –

including the US, Britain and the renowned Nigerian Nobel literature laureate, Wole Soyinka – to lead a campaign of diplomatic and economic sanctions against the Abacha regime. Instead, it opted for 'quiet' and 'cautious' diplomacy and a strategy of 'constructive engagement' until November 1995, when Ken Saro-Wiwa and eight other Ogoni minority-rights activists were executed.

Personally stung by the Nigerian government's refusal to heed international calls for clemency, including his own, Mandela expressed his outrage at a Commonwealth Heads of Government Meeting (CHOGM) in Auckland, New Zealand, and called for tougher measures including the expulsion of Nigeria from the Commonwealth and the imposition of an oil embargo. In uncharacteristic language, he warned Abacha that 'he is sitting on a volcano and I am going to explode it under him'. However, South Africa's call for sanctions was not heeded; its failure to galvanise support damaged the country's prestige and national pride, and cast it as 'pro-Western' and 'un-African' in the eyes of other African states.[39] It was the only developing country to recall its chief diplomatic representative, leading to accusations that it was breaching African solidarity. The OAU even castigated South Africa's sanctions call as 'not an African way to deal with an African problem'.[40] Moreover, within Africa the country was perceived as having been hoodwinked by Western governments with dubious motives, notably the US and Britain, into leading an unpopular campaign. In December 1995, the SADC heads of state decided that no further steps would be taken against Nigeria; the matter would be left to the eight-member Commonwealth Ministerial Action Group.[41]

The implosion of Zaire

In April–May 1997, South Africa attempted to broker a ceasefire agreement in Zaire between President Mobutu Sese Seko and Congolese rebels led by Laurent Kabila. This first foray into conflict mediation showed more prudence and measured judgement than the country's injudicious intervention over Nigeria. Zaire had been sliding towards anarchy for nearly 30 years, and it had become clear that the country's imminent implosion could destabilise the region. South Africa initiated a peace-building exercise in the hope of ensuring an orderly and peaceful transfer of power. Mandela hosted and led peace talks between Mobutu and Kabila aboard the *SAS*

Outeniqua, a South African navel vessel.

South Africa's motives and objectives were again ambiguous and subject to different interpretations. Was the intention to favour Kabila, whose long march to victory was nearly over (the preferred African option)? Or did Pretoria support a soft landing for the embattled Mobutu (the option favoured by the US, which had backed him for decades)?[42] Kabila, with the support of East African allies and Angola and with outright victory in sight, was less enamoured by Mandela's personal diplomacy and refused to settle for anything less than Mobutu's immediate departure from Kinshasa. Kabila seized the presidency in May 1997.

Bold though they were, South Africa's mediation efforts failed to deliver a peaceful and negotiated transition.[43] In early August 1998, rebels backed by Rwanda and Uganda launched an insurgency in the eastern Democratic Republic of Congo (DRC), Zaire's successor state, in response to increasing autocratic tendencies and misrule by Kabila. Soon after the conflict began, Zimbabwe, Angola and Namibia jointly deployed thousands of troops in support of the beleaguered president. South Africa was outmanoeuvred, apparently unaware of the intensification of the war and its implications for regional stability. Although opposed to external military intervention, it endorsed the intervention as being in the interests of the region. However, it quickly threw its diplomatic weight and resources behind Zambian leader Frederick Chiluba's attempts to broker a ceasefire agreement.[44]

Intervention in Lesotho

On 22 September 1998, troops from South Africa and Botswana intervened in Lesotho (ostensibly under an SADC banner) to restore order amid mounting social discontent, political stalemate and a looming constitutional crisis. The intervention in the enclave, sometimes described as South Africa's tenth province, aggravated an already grave situation and resulted in a groundswell of anti-South African feeling. While it succeeded in returning Lesotho's soldiers to their barracks, it was accompanied by widespread looting and destruction of property, especially in the capital, Maseru. In addition, there were at least 37 (and probably more) deaths among Basotho and South African soldiers, as well as Basotho civilians. Reports of abuses by South African troops led Amnesty International to express its concern to the South African government.[45] South African opposition parties and independent commentators described the intervention as a 'catastrophe'. Even senior officers within the South African National Defence Force (the SANDF, the successor to the apartheid government's South African Defence Force) acknowledged that ill-trained and inappropriate forces had been used and that the order for a military intervention had come as a surprise.[46] The intervention failed to comply with any of the criteria set out in the soon-to-be-adopted White Paper on peacekeeping.

Ironically, the South African government had dissociated itself from the intervention in the DRC's civil war by Zimbabwe, Namibia and Angola on the grounds that a negotiated solution was a better and more enduring option, and declared that South Africa would only consider intervening militarily in another country in the region as part of a joint SADC force acting under the auspices of the OAU and the UN. This position was undermined by the Lesotho operation. Although portrayed partially as a defence of democracy, it was clear that the South African government was more concerned about the security of the Lesotho Highlands Water Project, which was to supply South Africa with a significant amount of water, as well as the threat of unrest spilling over the border.[47]

Arms sales: a controversial test

By April 1994, South Africa had established itself as the tenth-largest arms producer in the world, with approximately 800 arms and arms-component manufacturers employing a workforce of 50,000. By 1997, weapons sales to 61 countries provided for substantial export earnings (R1.03 billion and an increase of 34% since 1994). Defence equipment had become South Africa's second-largest manufactured export, although accounting for less than 5% of the country's total manufacturing output, 1.2% of gross domestic product (GDP) and only 1% of all manufacturing jobs.[48]

Under the ANC government, there were great expectations for a new and ethical arms-trading regime. In September 1994, an arms-related scandal led the government to appoint the Cameron Commission to investigate South African arms exports and propose policy reforms.[49] In August 1995, following wide-ranging recommendations made by the Commission, the cabinet approved an interim arms-control policy that spelt out the principles and criteria governing national arms exports, including a robust human-rights dimension.

The government also created an inter-departmental cabinet committee to implement the policy, the National Conventional Arms Control Committee (NCACC), chaired by the then Minister of Water Affairs, Kader Asmal. The principles and norms of the policies were also incorporated into White Papers on defence and defence-related industries, published in 1996 and 1999 respectively. A government committee commenced work on a Conventional Arms Control Bill that would give statutory force to many of the political commitments made in these documents. In accordance with NCACC policies, the country refused to sell arms to a number of governments that would have been willing customers, including Nigeria under Abacha.

However, it soon became apparent that there was a significant gap between the theory professed by the NCACC and the practice of arms sales. Highly controversial transactions were made with the Rwandan government in March 1995 after the UN had imposed an international arms embargo, and with Congo-Brazzaville before the outbreak of hostilities there in 1996. The NCACC suspended the sale of weapons to Rwanda in 1996 amid fears that South African arms might be used by Rwandan forces to commit atrocities. But transfers were resumed despite an escalation in violence in western Rwanda and the involvement of Rwandan troops in human-rights abuses. South African-manufactured weapons were used by both sides in the war between the Sudan People's Liberation Army (SPLA) and the Sudanese government. In January 1996, the cabinet provisionally approved a R3bn contract to supply a tank firing-control system to Syria (to upgrade its outmoded Soviet-made T-72 tanks). The proposed sale provoked the anger of the US, which blacklisted Syria as a sponsor of terrorism. The threatened suspension of $120 million of US aid prevented South Africa from pursuing the deal. Other clients with questionable human-rights records include Algeria, Angola, Chad, Colombia and Indonesia. Arms sales to countries in conflict were strongly contested by the Ceasefire Campaign, a South African NGO, which questioned the efficacy and administrative rigour of the NCACC, which was apparently ignoring its own norms and standards when authorising transfers.[50]

Despite this troubling record, South Africa has played an important part in some of the key disarmament activities of the late twentieth century. As the only country ever unilaterally to abandon a nuclear-weapons programme, South Africa was instrumental in brokering an indefinite and conditional extension of the Nuclear Non-Proliferation Treaty (NPT) during the Review and Extension Conference in New York in May 1995. Indeed, as James Hamill and Donna Lee noted: 'The NPT conference was, in itself, a highly successful diplomatic venture for Pretoria and provides an example of a state punching above its weight in international affairs and playing the "bridge-building" or facilitating role between North and South with consummate skill'.[51] At the end of the conference, South Africa was key in defining the terms for establishing an African Nuclear Weapon-Free Zone. The country was also a leading player in the Ottawa process, which secured a global ban on the production and sale of anti-personnel landmines. In 1997, it was one of the first countries to enact a unilateral ban on such mines and actively campaigned for African adherence to the Mine Ban Treaty.

Transformation and apartheid's legacies

Less than a year after the founding democratic elections of 1994, South Africa had established full diplomatic relations with most states, including 46 African countries, and had been readmitted to full membership of the UN, the Commonwealth, the OAU and SADC. It was at various times chair of UNCTAD, SADC and the NAM, and chaired the fifty-fourth session of the UN Commission on Human Rights in 1998. On the eve of his departure from the presidency in 1999, Mandela declared that 'for a country that not so many years ago was the polecat of the world, South Africa has truly undergone a revolution in its relations with the international community'.[52] Its revived international standing could be seen in the acceptance of South Africa as broker of an agreement whereby Libya handed over suspects to stand trial in the 1998 bombing of a Pan Am passenger plane over Lockerbie in Scotland.

Yet a palpable tension remained between realism and idealism, between the country's perceived commercial, trade and political interests and its aspirational role as a moral crusader for human rights and democracy. The institutions of foreign policymaking were seen by many in the ANC to be unresponsive to the concerns of the majority of South Africans, and dominated in the middle ranks by old-regime officials. Reconciling these differing foreign-policy priorities and institutional tensions became an overriding objective of the incoming government in 1999.[53]

Chapter 2

Mbeki and the Foreign Policy of Consolidation

Incoming President Thabo Mbeki recognised that the contradictions in the formulation and implementation of South Africa's foreign policy could not be allowed to dominate South Africa's international conduct. It was clear, however, that any decision to foreswear the inchoate universalism of the Mandela period needed to be given further substance through closer engagement with multilateral partners in Africa and the South. There was a desire to reinvigorate South Africa's foreign policy with a broader continental – even global – agenda that conformed with the requirements of a developing country in an impoverished region, and with the normative precepts of Mbeki's 'African renaissance'.

Realising these ambitions occupied the early years of the Mbeki administration's foreign-policy development. Reconciling South African diplomacy with its domestic policies became a priority, coupled with a drive to consolidate the instruments of foreign policy-making within the framework of a larger reworking of government. Both tasks were aided by Mbeki's overwhelming political control within the ANC. With a close circle of colleagues at the helm of policy-making, he sought to develop a foreign policy with a stronger sense of purpose and vision. However, the move towards greater policy coherence and centralisation did not always result in better implementation or outcomes.

Reconfiguring foreign policy

Integrating South African foreign policy with domestic policies and capabilities was one of the hallmarks of the search for a post-Mandela approach to international relations. Although South Africa dominates the southern African region economically, in global terms it is a middle-income economy with a medium human-development ranking on the UN Development Programme's index, where it lies below Cuba and next to the Dominican Republic and Sri Lanka. Income inequality, which divides the country into a rich white minority and a poor black majority, is among the highest in the world.[1] Since 1994, jobless rates have grown, and more than a quarter of the working population is unemployed or underemployed.[2] Social problems such as crime and corruption have increased, and there are serious disparities not only between black and white but also between the newly enriched and ostentatious black middle class and a poor, mostly uneducated mass, and between urban and rural households.[3]

The South African government's response to these domestic challenges was to adjust its Reconstruction and Development Programme (RDP), which focused on poverty reduction and meeting the basic needs of those most disadvantaged by apartheid. By adopting the neo-liberal macroeconomic Growth, Employment and Redistribution (GEAR) strategy in 1996, the focus shifted to structural economic reform. This included fiscal reforms, the removal of exchange controls, monetary-policy discipline, the privatisation of state-owned assets, labour-market flexibility, tariff reductions and skills development. The GEAR targets were ambitious: it 'promised to increase annual growth by an average of 4.2%, create 1.35 million new jobs by the year 2000, boost exports by an average of 8.4% per annum through an array of supply side measures, and drastically improve social infrastructure'. The neo-liberal underpinnings were meant to be a catalyst for achieving 'growth with job creation and Redistribution'.[4]

The shift from RDP to GEAR had important implications for South Africa's foreign policy, since getting the 'economic fundamentals' right was meant to improve global competitiveness and export efficiency as well as inspire confidence among foreign investors. South Africa under Mbeki had decided to engage more earnestly and vigorously with the forces of globalisation as a means of improving economic growth, generating employment and addressing inequality. In other words, the market fundamentalism of

GEAR was seen as key for achieving the developmental goals that, for a variety of reasons, the RDP had failed to deliver.

The reconfiguration of South African foreign policy began in earnest in February 1999 when the new Director-General, Jackie Selebi, led an initiative that reformulated the DFA mission statement. This exercise, which brought together senior civil servants and heads of missions, as well as selected members of civil society, resulted in the promotion of 'security and wealth creation' as the DFA's new leitmotif and fundamental purpose. Security would be pursued through compliance with international law and active involvement in conflict prevention, resolution and management. Wealth creation would be managed through a balanced and coordinated approach to globalisation, the enhancement of South Africa's global image and the vigorous pursuit of trade and investment.[5] At the same time, Mbeki expressed his commitment to the idea of an 'African renaissance' (see Chapter 4).[6] Inspired by the pan-Africanist discourse of the 1960s, the president's vision for an African revival nevertheless introduced contemporary concerns around institutional accountability and democratic governance, coupled with a neo-liberal emphasis on foreign investment-led growth and open markets. Finally, the new approach emphasised the need for South Africa to champion the cause of developing countries by adopting a leadership role in multilateral institutions.

The emergence of GEAR and the promotion of wealth creation and security combined to provide a clearer, albeit contentious,[7] definition of South Africa's foreign-policy priorities. While human rights was an important part of policy under Mandela, South Africa had learnt, through its experiences with Nigeria and East Timor and in its arms sales to countries with dubious human-rights records, that principled rectitude and idealist leanings were difficult to sustain. As Gillies has shown, middle powers such as Canada, the Netherlands and Norway have been able to promote a culture of humane internationalism tied to human rights and democratic development precisely because they devote substantial political and economic resources to the project.[8] The Development Assistance Committee of the Organisation for Economic Cooperation and Development (OECD) is unequivocal 'about the potential for negative measures affecting the volume and form of their aid, in areas of serious and systematic violations of human rights and brutal reversals from democratisation'.[9] Even with Mandela's moral stature, South Africa did not possess such leverage. There would, therefore, be a gradual retrenchment of human-rights concerns under Mbeki; instead, South Africa's advocacy and support for human rights should occur through multilateral institutions and quiet bilateral diplomacy. The new neo-liberal orthodoxy coupled with a greater developmental focus to address historic injustices was seen to provide a better calculus of South Africa's national interests.[10]

Decision-making structures: the changing bureaucratic context

Following Mbeki's inauguration in June 1999, several changes were made to the national bureaucratic and policymaking machinery. Key to these was a belief in the need for a restructured presidency – the locus of foreign-policy formulation and decision-making. Careful planning went into the restructuring process, which had been initiated in 1996 in the wake of the closure of the RDP office and the shift to the GEAR strategy.[11] The restructuring has a direct bearing on the conduct of foreign policy, and what some perceive as the centralising tendencies of Mbeki's administration.[12]

The new 'integrated governance' system aimed to provide 'efficient and effective management of government by the president together with the deputy-president and cabinet'.[13] The president, deputy president and minister without portfolio are brought together in the same office with an integrated administrative establishment managed by one director-general (DG). Their work is supported by seven cabinet committees: social sector; economic sector; investment and employment; international relations; peace and security; justice, crime prevention and security; and governance and administration.[14] To ensure that cabinet decisions are translated into practical policy and legislation, the functions of DGs were also reorganised into clusters.[15]

The president's office is supported by a sophisticated administrative apparatus that includes the private offices of the president and the deputy president, the cabinet office and the Policy Coordination and Advisory Services (PCAS) unit. The latter two branches play an important role in foreign-policy decision-making. With the assistance of the PCAS unit, the cabinet operations chief directorate assesses the content of matters to be tabled within the cabinet. The PCAS unit advises the president (as well as his two colleagues in the presidency) on all aspects of policy coordination, implementation and monitoring, and assists on cross-cutting projects and programmes. The PCAS is made up of three chief directorates, which mirror the cabinet and DG clusters:

- governance and administration, which services the DG cluster and cabinet committee on governance and administrative policy matters;
- International Relations, Peace and Security (IRPS), which manages all matters related to international relations, trade, international investments, the marketing of South Africa abroad, and peace and security; and
- the economic cluster, which is concerned with economic, investment and employment issues, as well as human-resource development. It is also responsible for facilitating meetings with business, and with the International Investment Advisory Council (which includes figures such as the financier George Soros).[16]

The new system in operation: the enhanced presidency and the conduct of international relations

Within a year of taking office, the DG, Selebi, had fallen out with the new foreign minister and controversial former minister of health,[17] Nkosazana Dlamini-Zuma, and was replaced by Sipho Pityana, an official from the Department of Labour.[18] Deputy Foreign Minister Aziz Pahad remained in the post. The foreign minister and her deputy, and the DG and his, all hailed from the same ANC school, and were linked to the real foreign-policy architect, the president himself (whose work was supported by four special advisers for legal, political, economic and international affairs). These foreign-policy veterans, political appointees and administrators were charged with introducing an increasingly complex management system at a time when the government had embarked upon a recruitment drive within the foreign-policy bureaucracy.

The first task taken up by the new team was to make operational the reconfigured foreign-policy aims in the integrated-governance system. In early 2001, the cabinet approved a new integrated planning framework to guide the strategic national priorities identified by the executive. This was based upon an IRPS strategic plan that emerged from a DFA Heads of Mission conference in February 2001, and would inform the budgeting process over the next four years.[19] It featured four 'mutually reinforcing' themes representing the South African government's key foreign-policy objectives, namely: South Africa's domestic interests; the objectives of the African renaissance; promoting an agenda for the south, and developing an equitable global system.[20]

Mbeki, who participated in the DFA conference, focused in his presentations on the role South Africa was expected to play within the region, the continent, the South and internationally. He elaborated upon the four key foreign policy objectives, identifying the following specific issues as priorities: the OAU/African Union (AU) and SADC's restructuring; the reform of regional and international organisations such as the UN, the World Trade Organisation (WTO), the International Monetary Fund (IMF), the World Bank and the Commonwealth; South Africa's hosting of major international conferences (such as the World Conference on Racism and the OAU/AU summits); efforts at promoting peace and security in Africa and the Middle East; and an analysis of how South Africa's foreign-policy priorities and goals were shaped and influenced by its bilateral relations. Finally, he emphasised the importance of South Africa's relations with the G8 group of states, and envisaged a 'G8 of the South', new strategic partnerships with selected African states and improved cooperation.

It remains to be seen to what extent the new system of 'integrated governance' and the accompanying four-year strategic plan will result in improved ministerial and departmental coordination and advance the country's foreign-policy objectives. In a hybrid presidential-parliamentary system such as South Africa's, where the parliamentary opposition has a long tradition of exercising legislative prerogatives of review, criticism and amendment, the restructuring programme held serious implications for parliamentary oversight and, perhaps more surprisingly, for the role of the ANC as a political actor in the foreign-policy process. As one observer notes:

> *The institutional losers in this reorganisation are parliament and the ANC ... The committees not only lack the resources to monitor government effectively, but also have no oversight powers over the PCAS and the minister in the office of the president. But it is the ANC as a political entity that has been*

the most negatively affected. As the president builds the capacity of his executive office, so the ANC's capacity dwindles. President Mbeki wants officials at ANC headquarters to be managers, dealing with organisational matters such as errant branches and building election machinery rather than political issues.[21]

Meanwhile, the influence of civil society on South African foreign policy visibly diminished with the onset of the Mbeki presidency. Despite attempts to institutionalise debate and discussion, the perception is that the Mbeki administration is aloof and unresponsive. This impression has been reinforced since the implementation of the 'integrated governance' system, because it breaks with the precedent established during the Mandela era and contemplates no role for civil society in any of the prescribed clusters. Another reason for the declining influence of civil-society actors is that, at the conclusion of the Mandela era and the advent of the Mbeki administration in 1999, the period of policy development (in the form of White Papers) had more or less come to an end. In the Mandela period, many academics and NGOs crafted position papers that ultimately became government policy. The Mbeki government, by contrast, was more interested in concentrating its collective energies on policy implementation and service delivery. As the government builds its own institutional capacity, there has been a gradual curtailment in the scope of intellectuals, academics and NGOs to influence government foreign policy.

It is ironic therefore that a process that had as its starting point the need to reconsider foreign policy in South Africa's domestic context and a concurrent drive for better policy coordination has resulted in an approach that is arguably less attuned to that domestic environment. Civil-society organisations with a foreign-policy orientation, so much a feature of the foreign-policy debates of the Mandela period, are not consulted as frequently and have become typecast as critics of government policy. There is apparently discomfort within the executive over the attitudes of party members who are critical of the GEAR programme, retain concerns with issues such as human rights, and complicate and denounce the government's foreign policy. The bedrock of government support, the people who voted for the ANC, are obviously the stated beneficiaries of the new foreign policy but, contrary to its aims, integrated governance seems to have increased the distance between the government and its citizens.

Assessing the foreign policy of consolidation

The South African government's foreign-policy objectives are ambitious. At times, they represent a strategic approach better suited to larger players on the world stage. Some analysts argue that South Africa has aspirations to act as a middle power in international politics, like countries such as Canada and Sweden.[22] Others maintain that the South African approach is typical of a semi-peripheral state whose hegemony is bounded by its accepted and putative benevolent role in regional and continental affairs.[23]

South Africa's ambitions have to contend with, and are tempered by, three factors. First, it is questionable whether the country has the domestic strength and resources to play an activist regional and international role, especially as a continental peacekeeper and in the reform of the IMF, the World Bank and the UN. Rising poverty, chronic unemployment, poor economic growth, a fluctuating currency and increasing xenophobia are interwoven in a fragile social fabric, impeding the realisation of lofty foreign-policy goals. For example, it costs an estimated R1bn ($100m) a month to maintain a battalion of 1,000 military personnel in the field on a UN-type peacekeeping mission. Although the UN financial system will absorb a substantial portion of these costs, refunds to the South African government will only be received from the UN several years after the original expenditure. South Africa can ill-afford such cash-flow constraints in the face of urgent social spending needs.

Second, the deficit in human capacity exacerbates the challenges of managing so complex a policy machine. Reform of the bureaucracy has resulted in gaps across the DFA because of retirement and, in some cases, the hasty appointment of ill-qualified individuals to key middle-management positions. In the words of one ANC foreign-policy veteran, the 'careerist' has replaced the apartheid bureaucrat of old.[24] In a speech to parliament, Deputy Foreign Minister Pahad hinted at this potential problem: 'The Department of Foreign Affairs lacks sufficient capacity to discharge its continental and global responsibilities. Although substantial progress has been made in transformation of the bureaucratic structures, there are still shortcomings that need to be addressed. We believe that greater priority must be given to human resource development and performance management'.[25] The absence of internal capacity has compelled the government to turn to NGOs for assistance in fulfilling its ambitions. South African NGOs played a major role in efforts to facilitate the Inter-Congolese Dialogue, for example (see Chapter 3).

Third, while the general framework of policy is much more coherent than it was during the Mandela years, there appears to be a disjuncture between Mbeki's global objectives – reform of the Bretton Woods institutions; deepening regional integration; the revival of Africa; a better deal for the South – and their normative basis. A world view driven by a belief that idealism still holds value suggests an absolutism that might be difficult to maintain. In other words, an ethical foreign policy requires 'balancing the realities of world politics with normative visions of how it should be conducted'.[26] Under Mbeki, the embrace of multilateralism as the preferred instrument for realising South Africa's transformative foreign policy was based upon a faith in its mutability and resilience as a springboard of global activism. In fact, international institutions have often proved imperfect means of attaining South African objectives as the Zimbabwean crisis demonstrates. South African foreign policymakers have grappled with all these problems as they have struggled to reconcile increasingly lofty foreign-policy ambitions with the realities of African and international politics. The next two chapters will explore the specific challenges posed by conflict within SADC and the Great Lakes regions, and South Africa's effort to marshal international support for a grand continental development programme.

Chapter 3

South Africa, SADC and the Great Lakes: the Challenge of Conflict

South Africa's post-apartheid foreign policy, though aspiring to a role on the world stage, will be judged on its ability to manage conflict and promote development in Africa. In this sense, the outbreak of crises and conflict in Southern Africa and the Great Lakes poses the greatest challenge for South Africa's foreign policymakers. The post-civil war reconstruction of Angola, the internationalisation of the war in the DRC, ethnic strife in Burundi and the mounting economic and political crisis in Zimbabwe, all threaten the integrity of these states, as well as regional stability and prospects for development. The South African government, with an explicit commitment to 'play a catalytic role in ending Africa's wars', has embarked on initiatives that aim to tackle the immediate causes of these crises, as well as working to address their more enduring sources.

Complicating South Africa's engagement with the region is its own history of intervention in regional affairs under the apartheid regime, much of it destabilising, and a desire by the new ANC government to undo that legacy through active consultation with other regional states. Moreover, the continuing ambivalent attitude towards democracy and human rights among key SADC leaders, despite an explicit commitment to these principles in Article 4 of the SADC treaty of 1992, has made South Africa's promotion of these issues all the more problematic.

Against this backdrop, the guiding principles of South African policy towards the crises within SADC have focused on three basic concerns: to keep SADC united; to work to resolve institutional problems within SADC's framework; and, where necessary, to use other multilateral instruments and avenues to pursue conflict resolution.

Keeping SADC united

SADC's central position in South Africa's post-apartheid economic and political strategy precludes the country from acting in any way that would undermine the cohesion of the organisation. The original impetus for SADC in 1992 was as a vehicle for developmental regionalism, reflected in the fact that summit meetings were the responsibility of the ministers of trade and finance of the member states (as opposed to traditional regional projects, which are usually the responsibility of foreign ministries). A strategic review of the organisation completed in 1997 did not mention the need for it to assume a security role, but focused on structural issues related to development.[1] The trade, transport and finance sectors consume the bulk of the organisation's time and resources. South Africa places great stock in the organisation's commitment to sign up to and activate the 1996 Maseru Trade Protocol, which opens the region to cross-border exchange, and which it is believed will set in motion greater development and create the conditions for regional integration.

South Africa does not want to jeopardise the realisation of these larger aims (see Chapter 4). But complicating the dynamics within the SADC is the increasing ambivalence felt by some leaders towards constitutional democracy. If a 'multiparty/single party/ no party' typology is used to measure democratic progress in SADC countries, a positive picture emerges. In 1989, only three countries had multiparty systems; by 2002, there were 12. According to Freedom House indices,[2] Mauritius, South Africa, Botswana and Namibia were 'free countries'; Malawi, Mozambique, the Seychelles, Lesotho, Tanzania and Zambia were 'partly free', and 'unfree' countries were the DRC, Swaziland, Angola and Zimbabwe. Furthermore, during this period the number of single-party states declined from eight to zero; South Africa became a fully-fledged institutional democracy in 1994, and only the DRC and Swaziland remained non-electoral autocracies.[3] This positive scorecard, however, masks deep fissures within SADC, especially with regard to peace and stability. Within the SADC region, these are 'prerequisites for sustainable development and democracy. Conflict prevention becomes such a precondition. A functioning regional security organ (within SADC) that would prevent conflicts could therefore be a greater prerequisite for the deepening of democracy than some of the purely economic objectives of the older SADC, that had little, if anything to do with successful conflict prevention, peacemaking or peacekeeping'.[4]

Mandela's penchant for unilateralism on questions of principle or urgency – seen in his apparent threat to withdraw from SADC in 1997 and in launching bilateral negotiations with President Mobutu the same year – arguably contributed to inter-organisational dissent.[5] Since 1999, the unilateralist approach has been overtaken by Mbeki's conciliatory tone, which emphasises quiet diplomacy and consensus-building between member states. A contributing factor could be the tradition of post-independence African leaders offering solidarity to one another – though Mbeki has spoken out against this in the wider AU setting – which remains a cardinal principle of African inter-state relations.

Working to resolve institutional problems

There have been important tensions within SADC around security, leadership, democracy and intervention in states' internal affairs. Security-wise, the problems have concerned the relationship between the Organ for Politics, Defence and Security (the OPDS or Organ), the Inter-State Defence and Security Committee (ISDSC) and the SADC chairman. The attempt to create an Association of Southern African States in 1995, which proposed to incorporate the Front Line States as a separate entity from the SADC Secretariat under the auspices of heads of state and government, floundered exactly on this point of authority and autonomy.[6]

The Organ was established in January 1996 to 'allow more flexibility and timely response, at the highest level, to sensitive and potentially explosive situations'. A summit meeting in June elaborated upon its structure by tasking it with 16 specific roles.[7] However, the nature and responsibilities of the Organ were subject to ongoing dispute. This became acute in August 1998, when Zimbabwean President Robert Mugabe used his position as head of the Organ to authorise intervention in the Congo (despite the fact that the Organ had been suspended in Blantyre in 1997). In response, Mandela convened an extraordinary SADC summit on 23 August 1998 to re-examine the decision. The South African position on the validity of SADC intervention under the auspices of the Organ centred on the belief that the Organ was not constituted as a recognised free-standing regional entity, but derived its position from its relationship under SADC.[8] Zimbabwean officials took the view that the Organ, like its predecessor the Front Line States, was a largely informal grouping of senior officials chaired by a troika of heads of state that operated alongside – but not under – SADC, and therefore had the right to authorise intervention.[9] Indeed, the joint South African–Botswanan intervention in Lesotho, which Pretoria claimed took place under SADC auspices, was arguably on shakier ground than Mugabe's action.

Since the split over the Congo, South Africa has been quietly lobbying the other SADC members to consider restructuring the organisation to bring it under the control of the SADC chair. A SADC foreign ministers' meeting in late 2000 announced that the security sector would be included in the overall restructuring of the organisation, and this was confirmed at a heads of state summit in Windhoek, Namibia, in March 2001.[10] In a clear demonstration that the South African government understood the role economic incentives had played in sustaining the Zimbabwean military in the Congo intervention, they proposed that SADC should develop a regional arms-manufacturing capacity – incorporating the Zimbabwean defence industries which have been key beneficiaries of the war in the Congo – under the auspices of a restructured Organ.[11] Through the diplomacy of Swaziland and Mozambique, in conjunction with South Africa, the dilemma posed by the uncertain status of the Organ was resolved through the introduction of a triumvirate mechanism (comprising the past, present and future heads of the Organ), and Mugabe was persuaded to relinquish his leadership in August 2001.[12]

The Congo dispute overlapped with broader concerns around regional leadership, especially regarding Mugabe's suddenly diminished international status with the ascension of Mandela. It was also complicated by a desire to find a successor role for the Front Line States mechanism within the framework of SADC. Furthermore, the commitment to democracy and human rights that features in the SADC Treaty of 1992 implies that there is a role for some form of interference in the domestic affairs of SADC member states that violate these conditions. SADC actions supporting elections in Mozambique in 1994 and in Lesotho's constitutional crises in 1998 were conducted in the name of these values. Yet it is clear that, beyond the structural dispute and the debate over lines of authority, there remains an unresolved conflict within SADC over the statutory commitment to the promotion of democratisation and human rights and the maintenance of established norms of sovereignty.

The South African government's commitment to a multilateral approach towards foreign policy provides it with alternatives to SADC: the OAU/AU, with its officially-sanctioned regional initiatives such as the Arusha talks over Burundi; the UN, with various initiatives on Angola and the Congo; and the Commonwealth, with respect to the crisis in Zimbabwe. All provide alternative settings in which to give expression to South Africa's foreign-policy objectives. Where SADC as an institution has been unable to muster a strongly-articulated position on a conflict because of the involvement of its constituent members, the South African government has been able to participate in other multilateral initiatives that actively promote its concern to bring about peaceful resolution. Although there was a tendency under Mandela to pursue unilateral initiatives, this was most evident in South Africa's action in support of UN-brokered talks in Lusaka to win the adherence of Jonas Savimbi, the former leader of the National Union for the Total Independence of Angola (UNITA) – the general opprobrium and/or failure of these measures has curbed this tendency under President Mbeki.[13]

South Africa and the arc of crisis

In November 1999, South African Foreign Minister Dlamini-Zuma declared: 'The conflicts in the DRC and in Angola constitute the biggest challenges facing our foreign policy and that of other SADC member states ... without the return of this long awaited peace we will not be able to promote the economic and social regeneration of the region'.[14]

South African foreign policy towards the conflicts across the region has primarily sought to use multilateral instruments, including SADC, in pursuit of diplomatic solutions. In Angola and the Congo, multilateralism has been the preferred approach; however, with Zimbabwe, proximity and history have argued for a much more nuanced form of engagement. Finally, South Africa's role in Burundi, initially instigated outside the formal government apparatus, highlights both the possibilities of South African activism and its limitations.

Angola

In some respects, the conflict in Angola is the least problematic for both South Africa and SADC. However, both failed to become substantively involved in its resolution, reflecting both the ability of the MPLA government to resist outside engagement and the weakness of SADC mechanisms of conflict resolution. The MPLA was recognised as the legitimate government of Angola by SADC and the international community, a product of UNITA's defiance of the peace process after elections in September 1992 and the concomitant shrinking of its external support base. There was considerable convergence between official South African policy and that of multilateral institutions. Under these circumstances, the thrust of South African initiatives, in step with SADC, has therefore been twofold: to bolster the UN peace process and to eliminate domestic sources of UNITA support within South Africa.

The relationship between the ANC and the MPLA is rooted in the experience of liberation struggle, and South Africans trained for military action on Angolan territory. This has continued to influence the tenor of interaction between the two countries. Angola had served as the primary base for the ANC's military wing, Umkhonto we Sizwe (MK).[15] However, the heavy-handed behaviour of Angolan security forces towards the MK (especially dissident members), the increasing unwillingness of many MK soldiers to fight against UNITA, and ANC critiques of the MPLA's authoritarian and kleptocratic regime, all manifested themselves in a tangible distrust between Luanda and the new government in Pretoria. This antagonism was exacerbated by the actions of the South African government, which urged accommodation between the MPLA and UNITA, as well as the lingering links between white South African mercenaries, arms merchants, diamond smugglers and Savimbi's rebel movement, outlined in the UN's Fowler Report. The result was that Luanda successfully resisted greater South African involvement in resolving the Angolan conflict, beyond support for the Lusaka Protocol (see over) and efforts to isolate UNITA.

On the regional diplomatic front, while the war raged in the Angolan interior, South Africa and its SADC partners pressed for a diplomatic solution to the conflict under the auspices of the UN. As the tide began to turn against UNITA in mid-1993, Savimbi declared a unilateral ceasefire and began exploratory negotiations with the

MPLA in Lusaka. The protracted negotiations, which were mediated by the UN with the US, Russia and Portugal, culminated in the Lusaka Protocol of 1994. The pressure exerted by South Africa, while sometimes out of step with the talks and seemingly oriented towards accommodating Savimbi's concerns, ultimately contributed to an acceptable settlement.

The history of South African involvement in the conflict continues to cast a long shadow. On the one hand, links between UNITA and the South African military, developed during the apartheid era, persisted, despite the change of government in 1994, and UNITA received arms and expertise from South African sources. On the other hand, the MPLA offered equivalent financial incentives to attract South African assistance. Ironically, South African mercenaries working for the beleaguered MPLA government are said to have turned the tide against UNITA in 1993.[16] As the ANC began to assert its control over the governing apparatus in Pretoria, it moved to end the arms traffic to UNITA. Furthermore, as revelations emerged regarding South African mercenary involvement in Angola and Sierra Leone, the government passed legislation outlawing such activity. The most interventionist role played by South Africa was through its support of the ban on illicit diamond sales (the so-called 'Kimberley process'), the proceeds of which UNITA used to obtain weapons and fuel.

In the wake of the resurgence of outright conflict in Angola and direct Angolan military intervention in the Congo and northern Namibia, the South African government adopted a more overtly critical position on the longstanding civil war. Mandela observed that 'when Angolan forces increase the pressure, UNITA withdraws without a battle. This is a disturbing sign. Savimbi is an accomplished guerrilla fighter'.[17] At the SADC summit in Windhoek in 1999, Deputy Defence Minister Nozizwe Madlala-Routledge suggested that South African mediation could play a role in Angola: 'South Africa remains concerned that negotiations between the governing MPLA and the rebel group UNITA offers the only hope for lasting peace in Angola'.[18] Despite the history of difficulties in accommodating Savimbi's demands, the South African government appeared to believe that an acceptable formula could be devised that would resolve the conflict. The death of Savimbi at the hands of the Angolan army in February 2002 seemed to vindicate the MPLA's strategy of pursuing a military solution to the conflict, which included shutting down UNITA's supply lines in the Congo and diplomatic isolation, rather than South Africa's preferred approach.

Congo

The crisis in the Congo is arguably the most dangerous conflict facing the region. South Africa's initial enthusiasm for Kabila led it to proclaim that Mobutu's ousting heralded the dawn of an 'African renaissance'. With an eye to its substantial resources, South Africa sought to organise Congo's inclusion in SADC. South African multinationals vied for mining contracts with Kabila, while South African government departments openly courted the new leadership with a promise to put Congolese finances on a strong footing. However, this initial optimism was misplaced, and in Kinshasa a thinly-veiled hostility emerged towards South Africa's role in mediation in the ongoing conflict.[19]

Despite the friction within SADC, all the key parties to the conflict signed up to the Lusaka ceasefire agreement in July 1999. This called for a joint military commission, composed of representatives of foreign and Congolese forces as well as UN Security Council observers, in advance of a UN military observer mission and the installation of a peacekeeping force. The peace plan envisaged the withdrawal of all foreign forces and the demilitarisation of the conflict, followed by a consultative process. This inter-Congolese dialogue would bring together all political parties and civil-society representatives to agree a transitional government, paving the way for democratic politics. The UN Security Council established the UN Observer Mission to the Congo (MONUC) in August 1999 with the passage of Resolution 1258. It extended its mandate twice thereafter, despite slow progress in implementing the Lusaka agreement. In January 2000, after an unprecedented discussion at the UN between all the belligerents, the Security Council authorised the deployment of 500 military observers and, pending the withdrawal of foreign forces, 5,000 peacekeepers. In April 2000, the joint military commission agreed on a plan for the withdrawal of forces to positions 15km from the front lines, with UN peacekeepers as a buffer between them. This was modified in Harare in December 2000 to a call for the disarmament of armed groups within the Congo and the holding of a national dialogue on future transitional arrangements.[20]

Throughout the peace process, South Africa has supported a negotiated resolution to the conflict – a stance that implicitly recognises the security concerns of Rwanda – and therefore supported SADC, the OAU and UN mediation efforts. Zambian President Chiluba's role as a broker of the Lusaka ceasefire was strongly assisted, diplomatically as well as logistically, by the South African government, which organised follow-up conferences in an effort to win all-round backing from the parties to the negotiations.[21] However, the OAU's appointment of Botswana's former President Ketumile Masire to facilitate 'inter-Congolese dialogue', a move backed by South Africa, proved to be a stumbling-block. Kabila identified him with South Africa's interests and suggested that he should be replaced by F. W. de Klerk and Cyril Ramaphosa, two figures that were anathema to Mbeki.[22] South Africa's close ties to Uganda and Rwanda also fuelled suspicions. These links had resulted in a surge in trade and investment in these countries by South African companies.[23] In fact, Mandela had used South Africa's close relationship with Rwanda to persuade then Rwandan Vice-President Paul Kagame to admit publicly that Rwanda was militarily involved in the Congo in a bid to kick-start substantive negotiations.[24] Matters were not helped by Dlamini-Zuma's forthright manner. For example, speaking of Chiluba's ceasefire agreement of July 1999, Dlamini-Zuma disclosed that: 'The ceasefire proposals did not originate from any SADC initiative, as they were a combination of bilateral efforts driven mainly by Zambia and South Africa'.[25] Behind-the-scenes efforts to replace Chiluba, who was engaged in dubious efforts to entrench his position as head of state, with Mbeki threatened to further divide SADC on the Congo question.[26]

The assassination of Kabila and the installation of his son Joseph as Congolese president breathed new life into the MONUC mission and provided South African mediation with an opportunity to assume a high profile. Joseph Kabila's support for a negotiated end to the conflict was demonstrated by his willingness to disengage government forces from the front line in accordance with the Harare plan, allow more UN peacekeepers into the country and accept Masire as facilitator of the inter-Congolese dialogue. As a result, MONUC was able to partially deploy its 5,000-strong peacekeeping force as foreign military units began to pull back or, in the case of Namibia, pull out altogether (though fighting continued in the eastern part of the country between rival Congolese armed factions and Rwandan, Ugandan and Zimbabwean forces). At the same time, the focus shifted to reviving the inter-Congolese dialogue.

With the failure of a meeting in Addis Ababa in October 2001, South Africa stepped in and agreed to host talks in Sun City in early 2002, at considerable financial cost.[27] Doubts about the sincerity of the Congolese participants had emerged in the past, as well as difficulties in identifying 'legitimate' representatives of political factions and civil society, and it was with great trepidation that the South African government embarked on the process.[28] The fact that some of the Congolese had sold their positions as delegates did nothing to dispel these concerns, nor did the continued fighting in eastern Congo and the grandstanding of some parties during the negotiations themselves. Mbeki sought to secure a last-minute deal as the meeting drew to a close: the proposal involved a largely ceremonial role for Kabila as president, the creation of two vice-presidencies filled by the key rebel groups as well as posts in a cabinet of national reconciliation (defence, internal affairs, security, economic affairs and supervision of elections) for opposition figures.[29] This was accepted in modified form (the powers of the presidency were boosted) by the majority of the participants, but was opposed by the Rwandan-backed Congolese Rally for Democracy (RCD), as were South African efforts to extend the dialogue process to win RCD adherence.

In the aftermath of the Sun City talks, the Congolese Liberation Movement (MLC) and the government in Kinshasa (as well as the bulk of the participants to the inter-Congolese dialogue) agreed to implement most features of the proposal, but this did not alleviate concerns that the war, fuelled by its participants' resource exploitation, would continue unabated.[30] Nor did it counter suspicions that the main Congolese parties had come to an understanding in advance of Sun City and had choreographed their participation during the talks themselves. Despite these concerns, the South African government soldiered on in its sponsorship of negotiations, which included another round of direct talks with Mbeki in Cape Town later that year and the intervention of South Africa's foreign minister at a number of meetings between the Congolese factions. On 17 December 2002, South African mediation efforts were finally rewarded as all the key parties to the conflict signed a power-sharing agreement which, despite persistent fighting in Ituri province, set the stage for the demilitarisation of the conflict to commence in earnest.

Zimbabwe

Of all the crises facing southern Africa, that in Zimbabwe most directly affected South Africa's immediate interests and longer-term ambitions for continental leadership. Bound by geography, history and economics, the mounting political and economic calamities in Zimbabwe challenged the government in Pretoria to a greater degree than any other foreign-policy issue. An influential report by the Africa Institute of South Africa (AISA), the result of a government-instigated mission to Zimbabwe in early 2001, characterised the crisis as one of legitimacy, expectations and confidence.[31] This was manifested in the erosion of the post-colonial political consensus, the deterioration of the country's economic situation and the failure of structural adjustment, as well as the active undermining of the judiciary and actions of the security forces under Mugabe. Underlying the crisis was a failure to address the colonial legacy of land distribution, in which 10m hectares of the country's most viable land was owned by 4,500 mostly white commercial farmers, while 18m hectares were owned by about 850,000 black farmers. Meanwhile, Mugabe, the country's leader since independence in 1980, was unwilling to contemplate relinquishing power.

Despite evidence that the problems facing Zimbabwe were deeply structural rather than symptoms of a passing crisis, there was every expectation in most South African political and business circles that Harare would resolve these matters in conjunction with the international community. The steady trickle of illegal immigrants across the Limpopo, the difficulties experienced in bilateral trade, riots by Zimbabwe's liberation-war veterans, strikes by public-sector workers, the drying up of Zimbabwean-sourced investment capital and the nascent political activism against the governing Zimbabwe African National Union (Zanu-PF) all warned of impending crisis.[32] However, it was the intervention in the Congo in August 1998 that transformed the South African government's attitude to Zimbabwe. This shift was motivated on the one hand by the recognition that military intervention in the name of SADC jeopardised the organisation; on the other, it was a direct challenge to South African aspirations to regional leadership. With SADC split between two poles – Zimbabwe, Angola and Namibia versus South Africa, Botswana and Mozambique – Pretoria's ambitions for regional development and its own role as continental leader were called into question. Concurrently, opposition political forces within Zimbabwe formed a new party, the Movement for Democratic Change (MDC), in September 1999 under the leader of the Zimbabwean Congress of Trade Unions, Morgan Tsvangirai. Even within the governing party there was open discord, especially after the costs of the Congo intervention began to take their toll on the economy.[33]

Despite its limited leverage over Zimbabwe, the South African government sought to mobilise diplomacy and economic instruments to bring about a resolution to the crisis. Isolating and acting against Mugabe, whose behaviour as a rogue player within SADC threatened the organisation's unity, was not seen by Mbeki to be a viable option. South Africa's trade and investment interests in Zimbabwe, its largest trading partner in Africa, were still substantial. Any economic sanctions would impose high costs on South African businesses operating in the country, in addition to their domestic political repercussions, the consequences of which were uncertain.[34] The fear of refugee flows and greater economic chaos across the region also stayed Pretoria's hand and influenced fellow SADC states. Finally, given the slow pace of land reform within South Africa, the ANC government recognised that it was vulnerable domestically on the land question. Constructive engagement, or 'quiet diplomacy' designed to induce Mugabe to change his policies, became the means through which Pretoria sought to exercise influence over events in Zimbabwe. The South African government ensured that the Zimbabwean economy continued to function through, for example, extraordinary extensions of credit in key sectors such as power, where its parastatal company, Eskom supplied the bulk of Zimbabwe's needs (though the potential for supplies to be cut off remained). South Africa also acted as intermediary between the Bretton Woods institutions and Harare, and represented the concerns of the government and business. This has been the case especially in the volatile area of land reform, where Mbeki has sought foreign financial resources to pay for the purchase and legal transfer of white-owned farms. The South African government entered into a number of discussions with Mugabe that, for the most part, sought to give public assurances of support while suggesting Pretoria's mounting concerns through private channels.

The surprise defeat of a referendum on a new constitution in February 2000, which would have entrenched Mugabe in power, was compounded by the results of parliamentary elections in June 2000 in which, despite intimidation and the death of more than 30 MDC supporters, the MDC won 57 seats to Zanu's 62. Following the elections and the spiralling violence that accompanied land occupations by so-called 'war veterans', disquiet within South Africa over 'quiet diplomacy' became more public. The opposition criticised Mbeki's failure to condemn Mugabe and the threat to private property posed by the land occupations, while ANC dissidents expressed concern over the suppression of trade-union activity and human-rights violations.[35] At the same time, pressure began to mount within South Africa's rural and urban black communities for a resolution to their own problem of landlessness. In a sign of the divisive nature of the issue even within the ANC, Winnie Madikizela-Mandela visited an occupied farm in Zimbabwe in April 2000 as an unofficial act of solidarity with the 'war veterans'. Mugabe's call at a SADC summit for black Africans in other SADC countries to launch their own occupations of white-owned farms not only highlighted the slow pace of resettlement programmes in South Africa and Namibia, but also raised the possibility of Zimbabwe-inspired domestic strife within these states.

Despite these constraints, South African diplomacy continued to work through SADC to address Zimbabwe's crisis. This has not, however, been very successful. Discussions between Mugabe, Mbeki and Mozambican President Joachim Chissano at Victoria Falls in April 2000 did little to dispel the sense of regional support for the government's approach to land reform and suppression of dissent. Neither did a SADC summit in March 2001, which again provided Mugabe with an effective endorsement of his actions. Only at the SADC summit in August 2001, where the tone of the final communiqué stressed the importance of respect for law and property in Zimbabwe, could the organisation be said to have begun to publicly recognise the damage that Mugabe's policies were doing in the region.

The UN, the OAU and the Commonwealth were additional multilateral settings for the pursuit of South Africa's 'quiet diplomacy'. In the aftermath of the UN Millennium Summit in 2000, South African officials attempted to secure an IMF package and British financial support for land reform, but the effort collapsed around the question of transparency and due process. The OAU empowered Nigerian President Olusegun Obasanjo to meet Mbeki and Mugabe, and Obasanjo became the first African leader willing to publicly criticise Mugabe's actions. A meeting of Commonwealth ministers at Abuja in Nigeria in September 2001 seemed to offer an eleventh-hour solution to the problem of garnering British financial support for land reform, and its results were swiftly endorsed by five SADC presidents; however, the continued violent occupation of land, harassment of the media and persecution of the opposition put paid to the deal.

With the collapse of the Abuja agreement, and the fall in the value of the South African rand by 40%, there was an apparent hardening of the position within government circles in South Africa. The International Investors Fund, a gathering of leading business figures and politicians, spoke plainly of the damage that Zimbabwe was doing to South Africa's investment prospects.[36] Any thought of using South African leverage over Zimbabwe's energy sector, however, had been thwarted by a $360m deal between Mugabe and Libya's President Muammar Gaddafi, who agreed to provide fuel in exchange for expanding Zimbabwean exports into Libya, as well as a substantial share in Zimbabwean parastatals and commercial concerns.[37] As presidential elections in March 2002 approached and the persecution of the media and the opposition in Zimbabwe intensified, the EU and the US declared that conditions warranted the application of sanctions against the Zanu leadership, a position strongly criticised by Pretoria. At the same time, at the CHOGM in Australia, South African officials (along with other African leaders) resisted efforts to secure a condemnation of Mugabe's actions by insisting on waiting for the Commonwealth Observer Mission's report on the March elections.

South Africa's position on Zimbabwe was ultimately influenced by NEPAD (see Chapter 4). Mbeki had devoted considerable diplomatic and financial capital to winning support for NEPAD in the North. On the basis of a series of bilateral meetings as well as interventions at the World Economic Forum, Mbeki, along with Obasanjo, addressed a G8 meeting in June 2002.[38] In the aftermath of the Commonwealth meeting in Australia, the British government, which had strongly endorsed the NEPAD initiative, stated that its support for NEPAD might be affected by events in Zimbabwe.[39] The Commonwealth Observer Group issued a strong condemnation of the electoral process in Zimbabwe on 12 March 2002, though the 50-strong South African observer mission, despite internal dissent, declared the polls substantially 'free and fair'. SADC itself was divided, with the SADC parliamentary group condemning the election and the Council of Ministers declaring the results to be legitimate.[40] A senior British official, speaking after the results had been released, declared that British Prime Minister Tony Blair was 'sympathetic to NEPAD but if Mbeki rolls over on Zimbabwe, British domestic opinion may leave him little room for manoeuvre'.[41] Washington was more blunt; the Assistant Secretary for African Affairs stated that, without South African condemnation of the elections, 'NEPAD would be dead on arrival'. The hostile response of the international community to the South African government's position necessitated a retraction of a piece attributed to Mbeki in the online publication *ANC Today*, in which the elections were described as legitimate. After failing to attend Mugabe's inauguration on 17 March (though Deputy President Jacob Zuma was present), the South African and Nigerian presidents met Mugabe and Tsvangirai to discuss the possibility of a government of national unity, a suggestion ridiculed by Zanu ministers and ruled out by Tsvangirai. Finally, the leaders of South Africa, Nigeria and Australia met in London on 19 March and recommended that the Commonwealth suspend Zimbabwe for a year. This was followed the next year by a continuation of the ban after the leaders of the three countries found that the situation within Zimbabwe had not changed significantly.

Burundi

South Africa's role in the conflict in Burundi, while falling outside of the SADC framework, is important as it highlights features of the South African approach to conflict mediation. As the effort was organised outside the state apparatus by Mandela, it underscores the range of possibilities and action afforded by a more activist approach to resolving regional problems, as well as the more general difficulties inherent in achieving South Africa's ambitious agenda for Africa.

The crisis in Burundi had occupied Tanzanian President Julius Nyerere and the UN since the mid-1990s. Burundi, like its neighbour Rwanda, has had a history of conflict revolving around ethnic tensions between the minority Tutsi and majority Hutu population. Nyerere's death led to Mandela taking over mediation efforts in November 1999. Initially he drew heavily upon the international community's existing efforts – though he also utilised the South

African and NGO sector – later engaging South African government personnel as the peace process gathered momentum, to put together a comprehensive agreement to end the conflict.[42] His forceful approach to negotiations revived discussions on power-sharing, the reintegration of the military and an amnesty between the 19 parties to the conflict.[43] The peace agreement, signed in Arusha in August 2000, provided the framework for a transitional governing arrangement allowing Pierre Buyoya to retain the presidency for 18 months starting from November 2001, while a representative of the Hutu parties would occupy the post in the remaining period. It also provided for the creation of two houses of parliament. However, further discussions hampered its actual implementation.

Another agreement was reached on a three-year political transition process in July 2001, but Hutu rebels rejected it and violence continued in rural areas.[44] Negotiations in Pretoria in August 2001 on a ceasefire failed.[45] Like the Lusaka agreement on the Congo, the agreement struck in Arusha broke with UN precedent in that it authorised a peacekeeping-type operation despite the fact that not all parties had agreed to a ceasefire or to the introduction of foreign forces. In this tenuous situation, peacekeepers would serve as guarantors of protection and stability while the mediation process continued. This exercise in confidence-building was adopted in the hope that, over the longer term, the dissident factions would find themselves increasingly isolated and be brought into the peace process.

Having hammered out an agreement, Mandela organised an international peacekeeping operation.[46] He had envisaged an all-African force, led by South Africa, that would protect not only the participating leaders during the transition, but would also reform the military. Mandela had kept the South African government informed throughout most of the process, and was therefore in a position to identify and assess South Africa's capacity to support any such operation. Despite the fact that he had been out of office for three years, Mandela's continued influence within the governing apparatus enabled him to win support within parliament and the requisite government departments in short order, with the result that R535m was authorised to support the peacekeeping mission (on top of EU funding), and 700 South African peacekeepers were rapidly deployed as part of a protection force.[47] However, the operation itself demonstrated the weakness of South Africa's capacity in this area, as the mission occupied half the SANDF's operational capability and required the reorganisation of units within the military which, due to labour-union regulations, were able to veto participation.[48]

Mandela's authority both within and outside South Africa invites comparison with his successor, Mbeki, whose cautious, consensus-making approach to crisis management has seemingly achieved few results. Furthermore, the apparent ease with which Mandela mobilised support within NGOs, international institutions and the government for effective action contrasted with the difficulties that Mbeki has had in securing equivalent backing within these circles. At the same time, in the view of some South African analysts, the ad hoc nature of Mandela's intervention in Burundi, which was not linked to any broader regional strategy and seemed to be predicated on no other rationale than 'because Mandela requested it', pointed to a return to the uncoordinated approach to foreign policy of the recent past.[49]

Engagement and disillusionment

South Africa's attempts to play a key role in the resolution of conflict within southern Africa have a decidedly mixed record. While South African mediation has had a positive, if not instrumental, part in underwriting ceasefires and peace agreements in the Congo and Burundi, continuing tensions (and sometimes outright violence) within these countries highlights the tenuous nature of the gains achieved. In Angola, South Africa's role has been constrained by its past involvement, and Zimbabwe's slide into economic chaos, political tyranny and starvation has proved to be a major setback for South African diplomacy. Despite consistency of purpose, southern Africa has been remarkably resistant to South African efforts. The same is likely to be the case with potential conflicts in Mozambique, where the governing Frelimo party has resisted even limited power-sharing with an opposition that commands nearly 50% of the electorate's support, or the debates around the extension of presidential terms of office in Malawi and Namibia.

This audit of South African regional engagement highlights the difficulties Pretoria faces in realising its ambitious foreign-policy agenda for Africa. First, the decision to foreswear unilateralism in favour of multilateral approaches has had unexpected implications for South African foreign-policy choices. Whereas concerns for democracy and human rights featured in the debate on foreign policy in the immediate post-apartheid period, recourse to SADC – despite its formal commitment to these issues – has tended to circumscribe substantive action in support of these values. This in turn has had a direct effect upon the tools available to policymakers in Pretoria, limiting them to public statements through SADC that emphasised organisational cohesion over concern or condemnation of the actions of fellow members.[50] Furthermore, for the South African state, the hurdles to the effective implementation of foreign policy remain determined by administrative and analytical capacity as well as financial means, all of which are in relatively short supply.

Southern Africa, thought to be the region where South Africa could most readily exercise its influence, has proven a much more problematic theatre than expected. The determination of the leadership in Angola and (until Kabila's death) the Congo to resist any outside interference, especially by South Africa, shut Pretoria out of an area where it had hoped to play a constructive role. Even in those crises – Zimbabwe in particular – where South African interests were most directly effected and leverage was assumed to be considerable, the range of actions available that would not exact costs in terms of SADC unity, domestic politics and relations with G8 countries, turned out to be far smaller than policymakers in Pretoria had anticipated. By adopting the 'quiet-diplomacy' approach towards Zimbabwe, Mbeki had hoped to underscore the limitations of South Africa's willingness to overtly challenge the non-interventionist norm in SADC, while arguing that it was respecting the fact (flawed though it was) that Mugabe and Zanu had been democratically elected. But the rising chorus of international condemnation of Mbeki's position and its uncomfortable spill-over into South African politics brought about unanticipated pressures to shift policy in new directions. The contradictions between the self-imposed constraints of a 'benign' hegemon, for whom regional consensus was preferred over the naked exercise of power, and the aspirational politics of South Africa as a middle power with a self-proclaimed transformative destiny for the continent, continue to shape its diplomacy in Africa.

Chapter 4

South Africa, Africa and the South: Leadership and Revival

Southern Africa, Africa and the South form the regional axes of South Africa's post-apartheid foreign policy. While the management and resolution of conflict represents one crucial aspect of this policy, it is partnered with a desire to play a leadership role through the promotion of an ambitious agenda for regional and continental development. Faced with economic and political upheaval in these areas, coupled with the impact of globalisation, South African diplomacy has sought to reconstruct and revive regional institutions to meet the challenges of the twenty-first century. Central to this effort is Mbeki's call for an 'African renaissance', emphasising African responsibility for transforming the continent, which has inspired leaders of the North to give unprecedented consideration to South African-instigated plans for Africa's revival. Concurrently, South African officials have sought to use an activist approach to multilateralism as a means of redressing the global imbalances that plague Africa and the South in general.

South Africa and Southern Africa

It has become an axiom of South Africa's foreign policy that its own development and nation-building project is entwined with the reconstruction and revitalisation of the southern African region. Where it was once engaged in a destructive campaign of regional destabilisation[1] and inter-state hostilities during the apartheid era, South Africa now embraces a cooperative philosophy and professed intention 'to become part of a movement to create a new form of economic interaction in the region based on principles of mutual benefit and interdependence'.[2] In spite of the change in government, outlook and rhetoric, the dynamics of South Africa's relationship with SADC remain profoundly shaped by the contours of its dominant economic position and the influence of its business community.

Regionalisation in southern Africa is highly skewed, with South Africa historically acting as the hub and main beneficiary. As Dan O'Meara explains:

> *The central pole of accumulation was the mining and later agricultural, industrial and service sectors of the South African economy. All other countries in the region, except that of Angola, were locked into this regional economy as suppliers of cheap migrant labour, certain goods and services (water, energy, transport, etc) to the South African economy, and as markets for its manufactures and capital.*[3]

These unequal patterns of exchange bedevil integrative efforts. South Africa's GDP of $121bn, for example, amounts to three-quarters of the total GDP of the 13 other members of SADC. The regional market is of great current and potential importance to South Africa's economy, particularly its manufacturing sector. In 1990, South Africa supplied more than 80% of those countries' imports. Severely distorted trade relationships persist, with South Africa maintaining a very large trade balance in its favour. Its visible exports to the region have remained at more than seven times the level of imports.[4]

This state of affairs reflects not only South Africa's superior productive capacities, but also century-long efforts to establish and sustain its economic, political and military dominance in the region. This has been cemented by bilateral and multilateral agreements that without exception have favoured South Africa. Theoretically, the Southern African Customs Union (SACU)[5] provides for free trade between member countries, but South Africa has been historically the preferred investment destination and as a result this has stifled the development of their manufacturing industries. The Common Monetary Area established the South African rand as the common trading currency, effectively handing macroeconomic control over regional monetary and financial matters to South Africa. Levels of development among its neighbours are stunted,[6] and the legacy of apartheid destabilisation persists.

Reflecting the positive: South Africa as a regional pivot

South Africa's decision to embark on an export-led growth strategy is reinforcing the importance of African markets for its economy. In terms of total trade, South Africa's largest trading partner is the EU.[7] But its biggest export market is SADC. This is often overlooked when surveying South Africa's trade figures, the reason being that a great portion of South Africa's exports to other countries are 'hidden' within SACU. Once SACU figures are disaggregated, South Africa's 'exports to SADC in 1994 and 1995 were larger than those to the EU and its exports to non-SACU SADC countries almost doubled between 1993 and 1996'.[8] The size, comparative sophistication and diversity of the South African economy is also registered in capital flows. It attracts a larger and more varied share of capital flows than any other country in SADC. According to the World Bank, South Africa attracted more than $5bn in private capital flows in 1997 (including loans, portfolio investments and foreign direct investment), making it the most favoured destination in all of sub-Saharan Africa.[9] South Africa's large share of private capital flows and the size of its economy make it potentially an important source of investment into neighbouring countries. It has the most developed telecommunications system in the region and the largest and most sophisticated transport networks. In all of these respects, South Africa is the developmental hub of the region as well as a regional power. But given its contradictory impulses, the question remains whether South Africa can become the dynamic power in a region suffering from chronic conflict, under-development and poverty. The stated intention of its own policy-makers since the outset of the democratic transition is to play a benevolent role in the regionalisation process.[10] The challenge remains to reshape regional relationships in ways that yield mutual benefits.

For South Africa, the benefits of closer cooperation are self-evident. Joint and coordinated investment projects offer some hope for achieving economies of scale within the region. The 1996 Trade Protocol sets out to create a free-trade area though the absence of a coherent industrial strategy tends to reinforce South Africa's leading regional position. Combined with stronger political cooperation, coordinated trade reforms and synchronised investment policies, this could provide the region with better leverage when bargaining with multilateral institutions such as the WTO and the IFIs. Sharing unevenly spread managerial, professional, scientific, technological and natural resources – all part of the Mbeki agenda – could remove several barriers to the revival of more equitable development efforts in the region. The inclusion of social charters in agreements and protocols helps to expand the rights and conditions of workers and extend democratic practices in the region. Generally, South Africa's grand design is aimed at overcoming existing imbalances and inequities throughout the region. This could assist in remedying individual states' weaknesses vis-a-vis the North. They are essential if the endemic political and economic insecurities of the region are to be addressed. These include mass migration, refugee movements, organised crime, political instability, corruption and conflict.

Given South Africa's defining role in the skewed social and economic architecture of the region, any attempt to revise the regional architecture will depend upon winning Pretoria's support. In far-reaching respects, South Africa's role in southern African regionalisation is characterised by a mix of market-driven imperatives that reinforce and extend historical imbalances and disparities, as well as efforts by the new South African government to contribute to a more equitable form of regional integration. It is therefore not surprising that there is disquiet in some countries in the region, which have had their local industries either bought out by South African capital or undermined by lower-priced South African commodities, or have seen their retail markets dominated by South African firms and goods.[11] Even an ideal alternative to the current format of regionalism would remain premised on South Africa's dominance in most political and economic activities, and any effort to shift regionalisation onto a more equitable and progressive footing will have to contend with this. That South Africa is the leading regional power is less important than how it chooses to use that power.

Reflecting the negative: tensions within SADC

The family of SADC members is not a happy one. There are several sources of tension and acrimony that warrant attention. The most politically significant discord is between South Africa and Zimbabwe, while concerns linger about South Africa's ill-fated military intervention in Lesotho in September 1998. Since Zimbabwe's independence in 1980, its relations with South Africa have been strained. During the apartheid era of 1980–94, Zimbabwe was the leading front line state against South Africa's aggression in the region.[12]

SADC's predecessor, the Southern African Development Coordination Conference (SADCC), founded in 1980, had as its primary purpose reducing the region's economic and political dependence on South Africa by acting as a channel and coordinating mechanism for international aid and investment. Formal economic integration was not part of its mandate. When trade was diverted from South Africa, Zimbabwean manufactured exports replaced them.

As the largest and most diversified economy of the period, Zimbabwe enjoyed considerable political influence in the region. With South Africa's rehabilitation as a regional citizen and the emergence of Mandela as a statesman nonpareil, Mugabe suffered a loss of status and prestige, and this was at the root of the more visible disputes between the two countries over trade, investment and SADC's institutions of governance. Tensions were exacerbated in 1992 with the lapse of South Africa's preferential bilateral trade agreement with Zimbabwe. Under pressure from South African manufacturers, the government imposed tariffs on many Zimbabwean goods, including duties as high as 90% on textiles and garments. Negotiations to resolve the trade dispute proved unproductive, and in 1996 Zimbabwe implemented wide-ranging tariff increases on South African exports. Illegal immigration adds a complicating factor, as it does with many other SADC countries. Contrary to expectations, South Africa's much-vaunted GEAR strategy has not created employment opportunities. Unemployed and indigent illegal migrants from the region – especially from Zimbabwe, Zambia and Mozambique – have sought refuge in South Africa. In the process, xenophobia, particularly among South Africa's urban unemployed and informal sector, has increased. This simmering tension does not bode well for SADC's future. It was compounded by Mugabe's protracted and costly military involvement in the war in the DRC[13] and international pressure on Mbeki to be more assertive in halting Mugabe's slide into authoritarianism.[14]

In 1998, South Africa and Botswana joined forces under a SADC banner ostensibly to restore order and stability in Lesotho.

The intervention, which resembled a peace-enforcement operation, has been fraught with controversy. It was meant to neutralise the Lesotho army and to compel the parties to reach a negotiated settlement. However, the adventure exposed South Africa as less than a friendly neighbour. The impact of the intervention on Lesotho's already tense society and fragile economy cannot be exaggerated, and leaves its territorial integrity and sovereignty in a tenuous state.[15] For critics, this intervention demonstrates the continued salience of South Africa's traditional considerations of strategic interest, expediency and pragmatism over the human-security considerations which were supposed to inform its new foreign policy. South Africa, therefore, stands accused of not showing a clear commitment to equity and mutual benefit in the region.[16]

South Africa and the African continent

The tenor for the discourse about the African renaissance was set when Mbeki, then the deputy president, delivered an exultant address to parliament in 1996, in which he declared: 'I am an African'. This set the stage for a new mythic charter, conceptual narrative and normative agenda for what was needed to impel the continent's revival. Mbeki's speeches have been replete with calls for African leaders to observe norms and standards of good governance and sound economic management as correctives to past behaviour:

> *I have heard the stories of how those who had access to power, or access to those who had access to power, of how they have robbed and pillaged and broken all laws and ethical norms to acquire wealth ... It is out of this pungent mixture of greed, dehumanising poverty, obscene wealth and endemic public and private corrupt practice, that many of Africa's coups d'é-tat, civil wars and situations of instability are born and entrenched ... We must rebel against the tyrants and dicta-tors, those who seek to corrupt our societies and steal the wealth that belongs to the people.[17]*

Although Mbeki's renaissance vision generated intellectual enthusiasm at home, inspiring a surfeit of workshops, conferences and even the creation of an African Renaissance Institute headquatered in Gaberone, it largely failed to resonate across the continent.

There are several possible reasons for this. The first was the weakening of an overarching Pan-African idiom. Second, among African ruling classes and elites, it was viewed very much as a creature of a maverick who had yet to earn his credentials as an African leader. Third, among the more cynical, it was seen as a thinly-veiled attempt by South Africa to impose its hegemony on the continent. Fourth, its romanticism, replete with metaphors of revival, rebirth and reawakening, confronted the morbid symptoms and cold realities of Africa's decline: war, conflict, HIV/AIDS, poverty, malnutrition, drought and under-development. While the idea was not entirely abandoned – it remains an important pillar of Mbeki's foreign policy and a key orientation of his administration – it had become clear that it was an 'empty policy vessel'.[18]

Whether by fortuitous circumstance or design, a complementary development – the Millennium Africa Programme (MAP) – imbued the African renaissance with the continental policy buoyancy it lacked. Mbeki unveiled the framework at the World Economic Forum meeting in Davos, Switzerland, in January 2001. Bearing a distinct imprimatur of the African renaissance, the MAP focused on the following areas: the creation of peace, security, stability and the promotion of democratic governance; investing in people through a comprehensive human-development strategy; increasing investment in information and communications technology; improving the development of infrastructure, especially the transport and energy sectors; and mobilising sources of domestic and foreign financing for development.

Soon after the MAP was released, the President of Senegal, Abdoulaye Wade, launched the Omega Plan, which was widely seen as a francophone-inspired alternative and competing framework. Whatever tension and rivalry might have existed between the MAP and the Omega Plan was resolved through a deft compromise which synthesised and reconciled the two into the New African Initiative (NAI).[19]

With the endorsement of the OAU, the NAI, under the stewardship of Mbeki, Obasanjo and Bouteflika, Chairmen of NAM, G77 and OAU respectively,[20] appeared to enjoy the credibility and support of African leaders which Mbeki's African renaissance lacked. With the additions of Egypt and Senegal, South Africa, Nigeria and

Algeria constituted the core MAP Steering Committee countries, which jointly presented the NAI for approval to the OAU Summit in Lusaka in July 2001. This meeting was followed by an intensive lobbying effort with the G8, the EU, the UN and the Bretton Woods institutions. Another important development at the Lusaka summit was the establishment of a Heads of State and Government Implementation Committee to drive the NAI project. This committee has been expanded to 15 members.[21] They met in Abuja, Nigeria, in October 2001 to finalise the nature of the initiative and develop a definitive text. The same month, following a further round of consultations with African leaders, the Economic Commission for Africa and G8 counterparts, NAI was offically superseded by NEPAD. A management structure was set up, comprising the implementation committee, which was to meet three times a year and report to the OAU summit. It was to be supported by a steering committee, comprising personal representatives of the five initiating presidents and a secretariat, based in South Africa.[22] With the secretariat staffed largely by Mbeki protégés such as Wiseman Nkuhlu, much of the administrative structure and material presented by NEPAD reflects the concerns of South African foreign policy – the clustering structures of 'integrated governance', the macroeconomic concerns of GEAR and the lofty vocabulary of the African renaissance.[23]

The long diplomatic trajectory pursued by President Mbeki from articulating the African revival to the establishment of NEPAD was only the beginning of a process that required sustained engagement with the G8 countries. The 'enhanced partnerships' formulation at the core of NEPAD, which envisages the pooling of donor resources over a fixed time period toward particular states or regions as well as joint monitoring of progress, is predicated upon increased – in the short term – ODA and foreign investment.[24] Supporting this process is the African peer review mechanism, modelled loosely upon a similar fixture within the OECD, which provides for a voluntary submission of African governments to periodic review of adherence to transparency and governance criteria conducted by a board of African notables.[25]

The G8's response to NEPAD has been rhetorically positive but frustratingly short on substantive commitment of resources. For example, in a break with the recent past the United States and the

European Union pledged to increase development assistance at the Monterrey Summit in early 2002.[26] UK Prime Minister Tony Blair and Chancellor of the Exchequer Gordon Brown have spoken eloquently on the need for the international community to address African poverty. In spite of this, while NEPAD was designed to account for the diminished levels of foreign assistance overall as well as creating an enabling environment for foreign investment from OECD countries at the Kananaskis summit in 2002, it has not been able to attract more than $1bn of the $64bn sought by African leaders from the G8 and much of that was seen to be 'recycled' monies from prior commitments.[27] The Evian summit in 2003 was dominated by the Iraq War and additional finances pledged by the G8, including $15bn by President George W. Bush to combat HIV/AIDS in Africa, could not disguise the apparent slippage of African development issues off the industrialised countries' agenda. Perhaps more significantly, the unwillingness of the G8 to open its markets further to African agricultural goods – an act which would conform to the neo-liberal logic underpinning NEPAD – lay the foundation for a confrontation at the WTO (see below).

Overhauling the OAU

Since it was founded in 1963, the OAU has not proved itself capable of promoting African unity, despite the letter and spirit of its charter. It has long been a hostage to forces that it has found difficult to control. It reached it lowest point during the 1970s and 1980s, when coups became the preferred mode of leadership change. This was a direct consequence of the congenitally weak nature of African states, which 'were not forged by ethnicity, nationalism and war. They were simply bequeathed by departing imperial powers who left highly centralised, authoritarian states to a tiny group of Western-educated Africans who rushed in and took over … Independence often meant little more than a change in the colour of the faces of the oppressors'.[28] The OAU was unable to arrest the creeping malaise and paralysis in African governance. It was constrained by a provision in its charter that it would not interfere in the domestic affairs of its members, and would protect their territorial integrity and defend their sovereignty. This licensed, and in many instances exonerated, autocratic and unconstitutional behaviour on the continent. It was not surprising therefore that 'the broad African political class long ago decided that the continent had reached a point where it has to begin to move beyond the OAU. There is general agreement that the OAU has outlived its usefulness'.[29]

While the transformation of the OAU was set in train by the Abuja Treaty of 1991, which foresaw the phased introduction of continent-wide institutions such as a parliament and central bank ultimately resulting in the creation of an African Economic Community by 2028, the impetus for action came from an unexpected quarter – Muammar Gaddafi. Libya's disappointing experience with pan-Arabism and, concurrently, the willingness of African leaders to breach the international sanctions regime (for reasons of financial need or solidarity) imposed in the aftermath of the Lockebie incident, provided the foundation for a shift in focus 'southward'.[30] Colonel Gaddafi's willingness to provide the requisite resources to facilitate the transition from the OAU to the African Union, underscored by his action at the Sirte summit in 1999 and follow up meetings, gave the process a continued impetus that overcame the reluctance or scepticism of some African governments (including South Africa).

The OAU summit held in Lomé, Togo, in July 2000 adopted the Constitutive Act of the AU. The new Union is composed of the following organs: the assembly, as its supreme body; the executive council; specialised technical committees; the pan-African parliament; the court of justice; the economic and social council; financial institutions; and other organs which the assembly may deem fit to create.[31] In April 2001, South Africa ratified the act, becoming the thirty-fifth founding member of the AU. The AU was declared at the heads of state summit in Lusaka in July 2001, and held its inaugural summit in South Africa in July 2002. The veteran former foreign minister of Côte d'Ivoire, Amara Essy, was chosen as interim secretary-general, and led the year-long transformation of the OAU into the AU. In a related development, in November 2000 South Africa hosted a meeting of African parliamentarians where the protocol for the establishment of the pan-African parliament was finalised. Contentious and difficult issues regarding composition, jurisdiction and powers have yet to be resolved.

The AU's objectives depart fundamentally from those of its predecessor. In a continent renowned for bad governance and human-rights abuses, the act commits members, for example, to promote democratic principles and institutions, and to advance and protect its peoples' human rights. The good-governance discourse in the OAU was, in large measure, shaped by Mbeki. As early as the OAU summit in Algiers in July 1999, Mbeki called on Africa's political leadership to adhere to norms and standards of governance based on considerations of 'ethics, equity, inclusion, human security, sustainability and development'.[32] Through his intervention, in what was a first, the summit resolved to censure any future unconstitutional takeover of government. Mbeki has highlighted that African governments have to accept the need for change in their domestic policies in order to realise the goals of sub-regional and continental integration. The new continental architecture is meant to overcome the many structural deficiencies and institutional deficits of the OAU.

South Africa, under Mbeki's leadership, has used the opportunity to influence these changes to further shape its Africa diplomacy. It is therefore an irony (and in some circles an indictment) that Mbeki is reticent in taking strong positions in matters of bilateral diplomacy in sensitive and delicate matters relating to governance and human rights. This has clearly been demonstrated in the case of Zimbabwe. The logic of such bilateral 'silence' is that a multilateral framework such as the AU and its instrument of 'peer review' are better suited to handle such cases. It remains to be seen how effective the AU will be in policing the good-governance and human-rights aspects of its expanded charter.

A persistent difficulty in realising the rapid restructuring and launch of the AU has been the growing tension between South Africa and Libya. As the instigator and key financer of the AU, Libya has sought to influence the shape and content of the organisation to reflect Gaddafi's leadership aspirations.[33] The expectation that Mbeki would serve as the AU's first head, given that the inauguration would take place in South Africa, raised concerns in Libyan circles, where Gaddafi has been expected to assume a key leadership role in the institution; as a result, the AU's launch was postponed. Furthermore, strenuous efforts were made by South African officials to keep the NEPAD initiative administratively apart from the AU, as it was feared that the association with Gaddafi would damage support from G8 countries hostile to Libya. Exacerbating matters, from the South African perspective, was the crucial financial assistance rendered by Gaddafi to Zimbabwe during the build-up to the March 2002 elections, which undermined Pretoria's attempts to modify Mugabe's behaviour. In this sense, the decision to delay the launch of the AU can be seen as both a symptom of conflict over efforts by South African officials to imbue the structure with democratic principles, and as a tussle for continental leadership between Libya and South Africa.

South Africa and the South

Mbeki has made South Africa's solidarity with other developing countries another important foreign-policy priority. Their marginalisation and increasing poverty in the global system is of particular concern. For example, as its chairperson, he views the NAM as 'the conscience and the voice of the weak and powerless in the face of the dominant hegemony of the strong and powerful'.[34] During the Mandela years, South Africa used its 'moral capital' to build understanding and cooperation between the North and the South, notably as chair of UNCTAD but also as the chairs of the NAM and SADC. This approach has been reinforced under Mbeki after assuming the chair of the Commonwealth and in other multilateral forums.

South Africa's multilateral engagement is meant to address the more pernicious effects of globalisation by strong advocacy 'for a greater say by developing countries in global governance, for alleviating debt and other economic problems of poor states, and for reform of multilateral bodies to make them more sensitive to the particular needs of developing countries'.[35] The South African government has been active in developing positive trade and development agendas for African states, SADC and least-developed countries. Mbeki has been particularly outspoken about the role of the Bretton Woods institutions in perpetuating the debt crisis, and their undemocratic structures and practices, which militate against more open and participative forms of global governance.

Mbeki has framed the central thrust of the country's multilateral diplomacy as being: the restructuring of the UN, including the Security Council, a review of the functions of such bodies as the International Monetary Fund and World Bank, the determination of the agenda and the manner of the operation of the World Trade Organisation and an assessment of the role of the G7. Central to these processes must be the objective of reversing the marginalisation of Africa and the rest of the south, and therefore compensation for the reduction of national sovereignty by increasing the capacity of the south to impact on the system of global governance.[36]

Mbeki's multilateral agenda is very much driven by a collective search for global redistributive justice, and both widens and deepens the range of South African engagement initiated during the Mandela era. Under the Mbeki presidency, South Africa hosted the UN World Conference on Racism, Xenophobia and Related Intolerances in 2001, and the World Summit on Sustainable Development in 2002. Mbeki has also emerged as one of the key advocates in the global campaign for unconditional debt relief to Highly Indebted Poor Countries (HIPCs). Of the HIPC states, 33 are in Africa, and their estimated debt is $300bn. Using his position as chair of the NAM, Mbeki pressed the members of the G7 at their Okinawa summit in 2000 to live up to the commitments made at the Cologne summit to reduce the stock of nominal HIPC debt by up to $70bn, and he has used every bilateral meeting with G7 heads of state to remind them of this promise.

South Africa's trade diplomacy is also motivated by reformist impulses and is aimed at a strategic collaboration with a Southern bloc to change the foundations of the global trading system and to transform the WTO in ways that ameliorate the marginalising effects on developing countries. Indeed, 'within the WTO, South Africa has adopted a tactic that turns the tables on the dominant powers in the global economy and highlights their hypocrisy vis-à-vis "free trade" and "liberalisation"'.[37] South Africa's Minister of Finance, Trevor Manuel, has on occasion criticised 'anonymous' market forces, especially after the Asian collapse of 1997. These sentiments presumably informed the South African government's decision to take part in an initiative that led to the establishment of a 'Group of 22' emerging economies to examine ways of restructuring the international financial architecture. South African trade officials have sought to give substance to South-South cooperation through the promotion of special trading arrangements, with Brazil to the west, India and China to the east and the rest of Africa to the north (the so-called 'butterfly strategy').[38] Flowing from this was the creation of the IBSA (India, Brazil, South Africa) Trilateral Commission in the aftermath of their participation in the G8 summit of 2003, formalising relations and providing a forum for coordinating strategy between these leading industrial countries of the south. Their joint action at the WTO meeting in Cancun in September 2003 was credited with mobilising developing countries in rejecting the North's meagre offer on agricultural subsidies.

Promoting the developmental agenda of the South was a key element in Mbeki's participation in a number of meetings from 2000 to 2003: from the OAU–EU Summit in Cairo and G77 South Summit in Cuba to the MERCOSUR Summit in Argentina and the UN Millennium Summit in New York.

Assessing South African leadership of Africa and the South

A subject that provokes considerable academic debate at home,[39] South Africa's multilateral diplomacy resembles an evangelical crusade that is also reformist and constructivist.[40] Its achievements clearly rest in its ability to bring Africa's development back into the international public arena and, notwithstanding problems in getting them to fulfil commitments, to engage the top industrialised countries (and African leaders) in a common project towards fostering continental development. Indeed, without President Mbeki's visionary drive and South African resources, it is difficult to see how else Africa would be placed on the global agenda. The same could be said to a lesser extent regarding the revitalised south, which has benefited from South African leadership and more importantly the effort to reach out and coordinate action with other middle income developing countries. At the same time the terrain South Africa has chosen for cultivating its multilateral diplomacy is not an easy one. It will always be subject to cross-currents and countervailing tendencies where choices are made inordinately more difficult because of conflicting demands from domestic interests – especially with regard to democratic consolidation and social transformation – and managing international pressures where South Africa carries the burden of meeting high expectations to consistently punch above its weight. There are three concerns in this regard.

First, the South African government, particularly under Mbeki's stewardship, is often accused of being distant and aloof from civil society.[41] Foreign policy-oriented civic actors have viewed as perfunctory whatever efforts the government has made to engage them, a situation that has only been aggravated through the installation of the 'integrated-governance' system. There is particular unhappiness over Mbeki's multilateral diplomacy, which – it is felt by many South African civic actors – should reflect global trends towards incorporation of their concerns in both the development and implementation of policy initiatives.[42]

Second, because South African foreign policy is so closely identified with Mbeki, it becomes tied to perceptions of him. The international outcry surrounding Mbeki's views and policies towards HIV/AIDS has deeply affected international (and domestic) perceptions of his presidency. This trend has only been exacerbated by Mbeki's public equivocation over the Zimbabwe crisis. While the unprecedented international exposure given to the policy positions of an African leader is something that Mbeki courts in the name of advocating for South Africa and the developing world, the bad publicity that has accompanied his position on the pandemic has had a debilitating effect on other areas of South African diplomacy.[43]

Third, South Africa is still wrestling with the dialectic of identity construction in the global arena.[44] Under Mbeki, the country has certainly moved more purposefully – compared to the sometimes inchoate approach under Mandela – to locate its interests in Africa and the global South. However, suspicions persist about its bona fides in the region, the continent and beyond. For example, South Africa's historically close relationship with the US and Europe has resulted in institutionalised engagement. It is one of a group of select countries with a binational commission with the US and receives the lion's share of US development aid and investment in Africa. It has negotiated a free-trade agreement with its largest trading partner, the EU, which is seen as problematic for the SADC region. While perhaps a little severe, it is not surprising that 'South Africa is often accused of acting overwhelmingly in favour of Western, and particularly US, interests'.[45] The legacy of its past will remain an incubus until South Africa unequivocally projects itself as an African country with interests that distinctly reflect its own national priorities and concerns. As a cautionary measure, although there might be 'no reason to doubt the sincerity of Mr Mbeki's wish to effect change, and so contribute to improving the lot of many people in the developing world, he must be careful not to be set up as the ideological Trojan Horse of a seemingly reform-minded North, that is, instead out to protect its privileged position in the global economy at all costs'.[46]

Conclusion

South Africa and the Future

South Africa has successfully negotiated a transition from authoritarian rule to democracy, this transition involving far-reaching structural change in its domestic order. The country has responded to, and been profoundly shaped by, forces and factors in its regional, continental and global environments. The current realities of transnational interdependence make democratic transitions 'inescapably international phenomena … As global consensus on the desirability of liberal democracy has grown, the role of this pressure from without has only become all the more [of a] critical force in any transition dynamic'.[1] What has made South Africa's case exceptional is that, against all expectations, the transition itself was relatively peaceful and has ushered in a new government with an unusually strong desire to play an activist role on the international stage.[2] This acute sense of global mission, in contrast with other post-transition regimes in Eastern Europe and Latin America, is the product of South Africans' own sense of accomplishment in having successfully navigated the transition, coupled with the international expectations of its continental role, as well as liberation-movement idealism and residual solidarity politics.

South Africa's domestic transformation had to confront a range of difficult challenges and sometimes intractable problems, especially with regard to its full integration into international affairs. The instruments, institutions and processes of its foreign policy had to be radically altered to meet the demands and exigencies of a capricious and turbulent world, marked by 'the grim prospect of a retribalisation of large swathes of humankind by war and bloodshed', and conversely by 'a busy portrait of onrushing economic, technological and ecological forces that demand integration and uniformity'.[3] While foreign policymaking during the Mandela era was driven by a heady mix of idealistic and aspirational principles, it soon became evident that implementing these would be a difficult task, thereby bringing into stark relief the limitations which a middle-level country such as South Africa faced in advancing an ambitious foreign-policy agenda. During the Mandela years, South Africa resembled an overburdened and overstretched state trying to come to terms with this precarious and fragile world order. By virtue of its transition, South Africa was expected by the international community and many South Africans to be able to punch above its weight, a view that government officials tended to encourage. In this sense, the changes wrought by Mbeki have been inspired by large doses of pragmatism and moderation in recasting South Africa's role in a manner more commensurate with its size.

Acting in this spirit, Mbeki established a new set of priorities and normative principles more in keeping with South Africa's strategic interests and capabilities in the SADC region, Africa and the global South. This has resulted in a subtle move away from 'universality' to a more carefully-calibrated definition of how South Africa could focus its energies and resources. A broad and embracing framework of 'active multilateralism' now provides the conceptual and policy underpinnings for that focus, while not ignoring important bilateral relationships and collaborative partnerships with countries in the North and South.

Of equal importance, under Mbeki the machinery of government and foreign policy has been overhauled to provide for greater coherence and improved coordination among multiple state actors. The presidency, the primary locus of policy, has been entrenched through formal institutionalisation and a marginalisation of party interests, so that it now sets not only foreign-policy goals, but is the sole architect of an overarching foreign-policy vision. This is aligned to a global movement and ethos to address the plight and condition of developing countries, particularly in Africa. It represents a return to idealism, but one that is deliberately scripted in concert with the norms and values underpinning international institutions. Whether the new instruments and approaches of foreign policy under Mbeki's stewardship will contribute to better decision-making and stronger outcomes, much less its loftier aims to play a key role in reshaping current international norms, institutions and processes to champion global justice for Africa and the South, remains an open question.

Another significant consideration is South Africa's commitment to promoting a culture of conflict management and resolution. Domestic support for the South African government's commitment to conflict management in the region has held firm, for now. Where, for example, South African participation in peacekeeping in Burundi and the Congo raised local concerns, this has been more for their financial implications than any fear of becoming entangled in, as the opposition Democratic Alliance characterised it, 'a quagmire'. This view is echoed in the debate over funding the inter-Congolese dialogue in Sun City. While not especially featured in the public sphere, there remain concerns about the ability of the armed forces to successfully mount a peacekeeping operation. The debacle in Lesotho, coupled with continuing racial strife in its ranks, highlighted serious deficiencies in command and control as well as the incomplete nature of the transformation of the SANDF.[4] Perhaps even more crippling are the reports of HIV/AIDS rates among soldiers of more than 20%, the impact that this has on peacekeeping operations and amongst the middle ranking officers as well as the virtual collapse of training programmes and exercises (the last major military exercise being held in 1996).[5] Whether South Africa's other foreign-policy institutions are able to muster the analytical and administrative skills to conduct a sophisticated, integrative diplomacy is questionable.

South Africa's foray into strengthening regional security, through direct intervention, the mediation of conflict and institution-building at the SADC level, is strongly suggestive of the limitations upon its action. While having many of the trappings of a hegemonic power, South Africa is nonetheless finding it difficult to translate these attributes into concrete foreign-policy gains in the region. This gap between intention and outcome can be explained in part by the inadequacies within South Africa's foreign-policy institutions. However, there is considerable doubt as to whether any country, hegemon or otherwise, would be in a position to facilitate mediated solutions to the range and breadth of deep-seated ethnic, political and economic problems which plague southern Africa. An admiration for the South African impulse to serve as a broker for regional peace must therefore be tempered with a cold assessment of its failure to achieve meaningful results in Angola and Zimbabwe (and, to a lesser extent, in the Congo and Burundi).

South Africa's stated desire is to lead the continent in a revival through recourse to the economic programme embodied in the NEPAD process and the restructuring of regional organisations such as the OAU along more democratic lines. Here again, this is demonstrably difficult to achieve. Crucially, the ambivalence expressed by some African leaders towards Mbeki's initiatives – and, concurrently, an emerging critique within the powerful South African trade-union movement and amongst civil society in Africa of the neo-liberal underpinnings of NEPAD – has signalled the limits to realising South African reformist ambitions. On the one hand, these initiatives remain élite-driven exercises that rely upon the introduction of new structures and mechanisms of decision-making that are meant to enhance transparency and accountability in African governments. For Mbeki's approach to succeed in the short term, it needs to win over leaders whose inclinations are authoritarian (if not outright anti-democratic); his hope is that the benefits of NEPAD through increased foreign investment and aid will seduce leaders into participation. Conversely, if Mbeki is to succeed in his long-term ambition to reshape the economic and political aspects of the African state system, there is a need to transcend the emphasis on elite consensus and inspire African societies as a whole. The NEPAD initiative has yet to seriously engage civil society in the process, a significant oversight given that it is predisposed to support at least the governance dimensions of the programme.

South Africa's activist record in the broader international sphere also raises fundamental questions about the extent to which the global system is capable of being reformed under present circumstances. The principal axis of reform – North-South dialogue – has been effectively moribund. While the North obviously holds the balance of power in the relationship, Mbeki and a core of leaders who share this worldview have been calling on the South to reposition itself and exert more influence in recasting the international system more equitably. With variations drawn from his African themes, Mbeki has challenged the South to address its resource scarcity and supply-side constraints in a more systematic and robust manner. The governments of the South are therefore exhorted to focus on fundamental processes of governance; infrastructure and utility investment; minimum levels of social expenditure; and human capital development. In the wake of 11 September, a chastened North appears more willing to consider development concerns, and in this sense Mbeki sees a unique opportunity to improve the fortunes of the South through collective action.

While much can be made of the differences between South African foreign policy under Mandela and Mbeki – unilateralism replaced by multilateralism, for example – there is a case to be made for the underlying continuities that they share. The transformist idealism that was espoused by Mandela has continued, albeit in a different form, through its incorporation into Mbeki's reformist programme for African and multilateral institutions. The 'embedded idealism' proposed by Mbeki is predicated on the assumption that international institutions are open to reform and, crucially, that the leading powers and economic forces can be reined in through recourse to the universalist principles upon which they were founded. Indeed, in certain respects Mbeki's transformist agenda for the global system is more ambitious than the ad hoc universalism of the Mandela period. While Mandela aimed at particular targets as they arose (Nigeria, East Timor and the Western Sahara), the current administration has undertaken to rework international institutions and practices in step with new norms on sovereignty emerging primarily out of the Northern milieu.

At the same time, South Africa has attempted to reconfigure its foreign policy to reflect a new sense of its own identity as a leading African state, to target a new arena for activism in continental Africa and to rebuild a global constituency among the states of the South. Pretoria's ambitions are aimed at reshaping the institutions and, ultimately, the norms which govern the international system, while affirming South Africa's position within the framework of a state-centric sub-system (Africa and the South) that is often hostile to the imposition of norms that challenge sovereignty. This is at the root of many of the difficulties being experienced by South African diplomacy. Being 'of Africa and the South', but intent on giving expression to those distinctly non- (and even anti-) state notions which are derived both from the anti-apartheid movement and, more generally, from the post-Cold War North, places the South African government in an invidious position within much of the African political environment intent on upholding rights of leaders over citizens and the sancity of sovereignty over cosmopolitan values such as human rights.

It is this faith in the ethical foundations of multilateral institutions, coupled with a confident expectation of their basic utility, that guides South Africa's post-apartheid foreign policymakers in Pretoria as they map out the country's future. Yet it must be recognised that the idealist roots of post-apartheid foreign policy also impose limitations on action and continue to do battle with impulses that reflect South Africa's dominant economic position on the African continent. How far a transformational agenda aimed at regional and international institutions can succeed when South Africa seems unable (or unwilling) to manage crises in its 'near abroad' remains crucial to understanding the shape of its foreign policy in the years to come.

Notes

Introduction

1. As one observer put it, 'the grim prospect of a retribalisation of large swaths of humankind by war and bloodshed' in the post-Cold War era was matched by 'a busy portrait of onrushing economic, technological and ecological forces that demand integration and uniformity'. Benjamin Barber, *Jihad vs McWorld: How Globalisation and Tribalism Are Reshaping the World* (New York: Ballantine, 1995), p. 4.

2. Bernard M Magubane, *The Political Economy of Race and Class in South Africa* (New York: Monthly Review Press, 1979), pp. 323–30.

3. Stanley B Greenberg, *Legitimating the Illegitimate: State, Markets and Resistance in South Africa* (Berkeley, CA: University of California Press, 1987) pp. 177–201.

4. Patti Waldheimer and Michael Holman, 'A Powerful Spirit of Unity', *Financial Times*, 18 July 1994, p. 1.

5. Hein Marais, *South Africa, Limits to Change: The Political Economy of Transition* (Cape Town: Juta/University of Cape Town Press, 1998), pp. 83–93.

6. Nelson Mandela, 'South Africa's Future Foreign Policy', *Foreign Affairs*, vol. 72, no. 5, 1993, p. 87.

7. In March 1994, the ANC published a comprehensive foreign-policy document, which laid down the principles which have guided the conduct of South Africa's international relations. These were:

- a belief and preoccupation with human rights, which extends beyond the political, embracing economic, social and environmental dimensions;
- a belief that just and lasting solutions to the problems of humankind can only come through the promotion of democracy world-wide;
- a belief that justice and international law should guide relations between nations;
- a belief that international peace is the goal towards which all nations should strive;
- a belief that South Africa's foreign policy should reflect the interests of Africa;
- a belief that South Africa's economic development depends on growing regional and international economic cooperation; and
- a belief that South Africa's foreign relations must mirror a deep commitment to the consolidation

of its democracy. ANC, 'Foreign Policy Perspectives in a Democratic South Africa', Johannesburg, 1994.

Chapter 1

1 Donald Sole, 'South Africa's Foreign Policy Assumptions and Objectives from Hertzog to De Klerk', *South African Journal of International Affairs*, vol. 2, no. 1, 1994, p. 104.

2 See Chris Alden, *Apartheid's Last Stand: The Rise and Fall of the South African Security State* (London: Macmillan Press, 1996).

3 These countries were part of an important nucleus that provided the ANC with material and moral support on the basis of their ideological position in support of liberation movements in southern Africa, with the ANC being one of the most important beneficiaries. In its failure to transcend allegiances developed in the course of its global anti-apartheid crusade, the ANC-in-power has been criticised for failing to distinguish between 'party-government' and 'party-state' interests. Greg Mills, 'South African Foreign Policy in Review', in *South African Yearbook of International Affairs* (Johannesburg: South African Institute of International Affairs, 1998), p. 6.

4 See Mandela, 'South African Foreign Policy'.

5 For more than a century, South Africa has been a member of a customs union with four neighbouring countries (Botswana, Lesotho, Namibia and Swaziland), as well as part of a monetary union with three of them (Swaziland, Lesotho and Namibia). D. O'Meara, 'Regional Economic Integration in Post-Apartheid South Africa – Dream or Reality?', in A. van Nieuwkerk and G. van Staden (eds), *Southern*

Africa at the Crossroads (Johannesburg: South African Institute of International Affairs, 1991).

6 C. Landsberg and Z. Masiza, *The Anarchic Miracle: Global (Dis)order and Syndicated Crime in South Africa* (Johannesburg: Centre for Policy Studies, 1996).

7 African Development Bank, *Economic Integration in Southern Africa*, vol. 1 (Abidjan: ADB, 1993), pp. 277–317.

8 During the months immediately prior to the 1994 elections, a Transitional Executive Council (TEC), which included representatives of the outgoing National Party government and the ANC, was responsible for governing the country. A TEC Subcouncil on Foreign Affairs began the process of reviewing foreign policy and restructuring the Department of Foreign Affairs (DFA). This function was taken over by the new government in May 1994.

9 See, for example, D. J. Geldenhuys, *The Diplomacy of Isolation: South Africa's Foreign Policy Making* (Johannesburg: Macmillan, 1984).

10 The TBVC homelands had a combined foreign affairs staff of more than 800. Under the terms of a TEC agreement, those who did not accept the offer of voluntary retirement had to be offered positions in the DFA. Accordingly, some 415 were absorbed into the restructured department.

11 In terms of the sunset clauses negotiated as part of the transition, all white civil servants of the old order could retain their positions (this is how Director-General Rusty Evans kept his senior post at a time when the ANC needed one of its own to reshape and restructure the DFA). The white officials who stayed on in the DFA made up a very

influential centre of bureaucratic gravity, with a distinct worldview, operational style and view of authority. The ANC group's disposition and experiences were in the main diametrically opposed to this white, male-dominated old order.

12 Janis van der Westhuizen, 'South Africa's Emergence as a Middle Power', *Third World Quarterly*, vol. 19, no. 3, 1998, p. 444.

13 See, for example, the DFA's 1996 South African Foreign Policy Discussion Document. While other departments produced far-reaching policy white papers, the DFA was roundly criticised by academics and NGOs for not producing a systematic, action-oriented blueprint of foreign policy goals, plans and strategies. See Ceasefire Campaign, 'Rethinking Foreign Policy: A Response to the Department of Foreign Affairs Discussion Document', Johannesburg, 28 August 1996.

14 Christopher Hill, *The Changing Politics of Foreign Policy* (Basingstoke: Palgrave Macmillan, 2003) pp. 79-80.

15 Greg Mills, 'Leaning All Over the Place? The Not-So-New South Africa's Foreign Policy', in H. Solomon (ed.), *Fairy Godmother, Hegemon or Partner: In Search of a South African Foreign Policy*, ISS Monograph Series 13, 1997, p. 19.

16 Marie Muller, 'The Institutional Dimension: The Department of Foreign Affairs and Overseas Missions', in W. Carlsnaes and M. Muller (eds.), *Change and South Africa's External Relations* (Johannesburg: International Thomson Publishing, 1997) p. 69.

17 See R. O. Keohane and J. Nye, *Power and Interdependence* (Boston, MA: Little Brown, 1977).

18 L. Karvonen and B. Sundelius, *Internationalization and Foreign Policy* (London: Gower Publishing, 1987) p. 7.

19 Mills, 'Leaning All Over the Place?', p. 24.

20 The most authoritative and arresting account of his life is by Anthony Sampson, *Mandela: The Authorised Biography* (Johannesburg: Jonathan Ball Publishers, 1999).

21 Erudite, broadly read and perhaps reflecting his British academic background, Mbeki's allegorical and provocative speeches are often laced with quotations from Marx, Tawney, Byron, Shakespeare and Yeats. See *Africa the Time Has Come: Selected Speeches Thabo Mbeki* (Cape Town: Tafelberg Publishers, 1998), pp. 10, 12, 40, 87, 257.

22 Garth Shelton, *South African Arms Sales to the Middle East - Promoting Peace or Fuelling the Arms Race?*, FGD Occasional Paper 16, 1998.

23 See Raymond Suttner, 'Dilemmas in South African Foreign Policy: The Question of China', in *South Africa and the Two Chinas Dilemma* (Braamfontein: Foundation for Global Dialogue/South African Institute for International Affairs, 1995), pp. 4–9.

24 Marais, *South Africa, Limits to Change*, p. 205.

25 See John Daniel, 'A Critical Reflection on the GNU's Foreign Policy Initiatives and Responses', in Chris Landsberg et al. (eds), *Mission Imperfect: Redirecting South Africa's Foreign Policy*, FGD/CPS, 1995, pp. 32–38.

26 *Ibid*. South Africa's presidential system and the two presidents' overwhelming role in shaping foreign policy adds to the DFA's malaise.

27 Paul Williams, 'South African Foreign Policy: Getting Critical', *Politikon*, vol. 27, no. 1, May 2000, p. 73.

28 The tendency towards intellectual conformity is symptomatic of a lack of critical scholarship within the foreign-policy and defence establishments, leading to the

remark that 'post-apartheid South Africa has not taken kindly to critical scrutiny … Harsh responses to critics have discouraged most [ANC] aligned scholars and activists from engaging in any form of public scrutiny … Given this, criticism is becoming the preserve of mainstream and conservative scholars'. Adam Habib, 'Review Essay', *Transformation*, 37, 1998, p. 102.

[29] Jose Ramos Horta, 'Mandela Must Take a Stand on East Timor', *Sunday Independent*, (Johannesburg), 10 May 1998.

[30] Stefaans Brummer, 'Mandela's Strange Links to Human Rights Abuser', *ibid.*, 26 May-1 June 1995.

[31] Gaye Davis, 'For Sale: SA's Diplomatic Relations', *ibid.*, 8 December-15 December 1995.

[32] South African Press Association, 6 March 1997.

[33] *Ibid.*, 9 March 1997.

[34] The change was a consequence of three factors: 1) the continued refusal of China to countenance full diplomatic ties while South Africa maintained diplomatic relations with Taiwan; 2) the impending transfer of Hong Kong to China in July 1997 and the possible loss of South Africa's consular status in Hong Kong; and 3) the burgeoning Chinese consumer market and the potential for increased South African exports. See C. Alden, 'Solving South Africa's Chinese Puzzle: Democratic Foreign Policy Making and the "Two China" Question', in J. Broderick et al. (eds), *South Africa's Foreign Policy: Dilemmas of a New Democracy* (Basingstoke: Palgrave, 2001), pp. 119-38; S. Singh, 'Sino-South African Relations: Coming Full Circle', *African Security Review*, vol. 6, no. 2, 1997, pp. 52–59.

[35] South African Press Association, 6 December 1997.

[36] *Ibid.*, 13 April 1998.

[37] *Ibid.*, 9 December 1999.

[38] Maxi van Aardt, 'A Foreign Policy To Die For: South Africa's Response to the Nigerian Crisis', *Africa Insight*, vol. 26, no. 2, 1996, pp. 107–18.

[39] Gerrit Olivier and Deon Geldenhuys, 'South Africa's Foreign Policy: From Idealism to Pragmatism', *Business and the Contemporary World*, vol. 9, no. 2, 1997, p. 372.

[40] Denis Venter, 'South Africa and Africa: Relations in a Time of Change', in Carlsnaes and Muller (eds), *Change and South Africa's External Relations*, p. 94.

[41] *Change and South Africa's External Relations*, pp. 91–95.

[42] Peter Vale and Sipho Maseko, 'South Africa and the African Renaissance', in *South Africa and Africa: Reflections on the African Renaissance*, FGD Occasional Paper 17, 1998, p. 3.

[43] International Crisis Group, 'Africa's Seven Nation War', 21 May 1999, www.crisisweb.org/projects/cafrica/reports/ca05repb.htm.

[44] Roger Kibasomba, 'Understanding the Great Lakes Crisis: Whither the DRC', paper presented to the Africa Institute, Pretoria, 24 February 2000.

[45] 'Lesotho: Inhumane Prison Conditions for 50 Soldiers Facing Court Martial', Amnesty International, 21 January 1999.

[46] 'To a Little Kingdom', *Africa Confidential*, vol. 39, no. 20, 9 October 1998.

[47] Kabela Matlosa, 'The Lesotho Conflict: Major Causes and Management', in *Crisis in Lesotho: The Challenge of Managing Conflict in Southern Africa*, FGD African Dialogue Series, 1999, pp. 6–10.

[48] Garth Shelton, *South African Arms Sales to North Africa and the Middle East -Promoting Peace or Fuelling the Arms Race?*, Foundation for

Global Dialogue Occasional Paper 16, October 1998, p. 2.

49 Peter Batchelor, 'Arms and the ANC', *Bulletin of the Atomic Scientists*, vol. 54, no. 5, 1998, pp. 56–61.

50 'South Africa and the International Arms Trade', Report on the Ceasefire National Anti-Militarisation Conference, 17–19 March 1995, pp. 32–37.

51 James Hamill and Donna Lee, 'A Middle Power Paradox? South African Diplomacy in the Post-Apartheid Era', *International Relations*, vol. 15, no. 4, 2001, p. 44. Even Vice-President Al Gore added his accolades, saying that 'South Africa played a central role in achieving this important outcome, which will contribute significantly to advancing the security and political interests of all nations. If I may say so, your role in this effort was central to its success and displayed statesmanship of the highest order.' Cited in a speech by Alfred Nzo, Minister of Foreign Affairs, to the National Assembly, Cape Town, 18 May 1995.

52 Opening session of parliament, Cape Town, 5 February 1999.

53 The foreign-policy beliefs of South Africans reflect this tension. In the only foreign-policy public opinion survey conducted among 3,500 South Africans of all racial groups in 1997–98, 78% strongly supported promoting human rights; 75% supported a role in peacekeeping; 49% were in favour of participating in the UN; 62% supported nuclear-arms control; and 81% combating illegal drug trafficking. On arms sales, 39% supported sales to countries only with a good human rights record and not at war, and 48% were in favour of South Africa not selling arms at all. More than 45% supported the advancement of South Africa's economic interests as a foreign-policy priority. See Philip Nel, 'The Foreign Policy Beliefs of South Africans: A First Cut', *Journal of Contemporary African Studies*, vol. 17, no. 1, 1999, pp. 132, 134, 140.

Chapter 2

1 Marais, *South Africa, Limits to Change*, pp. 7–11.

2 *Ibid.*, pp. 100–105.

3 The number of violent crimes recorded by the police increased from 630,108 in 1994/95 to 839,639 in 2001/02. Rape cases recorded by the police increased from 43,962 in 1994/95 to 53,920 in 2001/02. Robberies with aggravating circumstances contribute greatly to fear of crime in South Africa, and follow the same pattern: 84,795 in 1994/95 and 116,736 in 2001/02. Sibusiso Masuku, 'Prevention Is Better Than Cure: Addressing Violent Crime in South Africa', Institute for Security Studies, SA Crime Quarterly, no. 2, November 2002, pp. 6–8.

4 *Ibid.*, p. 63.

5 Department of Foreign Affairs, *Thematic Reviews/Strategic Planning* (Pretoria: DFA, 1999).

6 Mbeki, 'The African Renaissance: South Africa and the World', speech delivered at the UN University, Tokyo, 9 April 1998.

7 See Leonard Gentle, 'The Tail Wags the Dog: Gear and Local Development', *South African Labour Bulletin*, vol. 25, no. 6, December 2001, pp. 71–76.

8 Gillies, op. cit.

9 OECD, DAC *Orientations to Participatory Development and Good Governance* (Paris: OECD, 1993), cited in *ibid.*, pp. 26–27.

10 Williams, 'South African Foreign Policy', p. 80.

11 The recommendations of a Presidential Review Committee, appointed in 1996, together with

the Office of the then deputy president, were implemented immediately after Mbeki took office, and were concluded by late 1999. For an overview of the process see Sean Jacobs, 'Remaking the Presidency: Coordination Versus Centralisation', Indicator SA, vol. 19, no. 1, pp. 30–35.

12 *Ibid.*

13 Frank Chikane, *Integrated Governance: A Restructured Presidency at Work* (Pretoria: Office of the Presidency, 2001).

14 *Ibid.*, p. 17.

15 *Ibid.*, p. 32. There are five DG clusters, one less than at cabinet level. This is because the DG economic and investment cluster serves both the economic and investment and employment cabinet committees.

16 Other structures and relations with the presidency relevant to foreign policy include: the presidency's consultative groups, which involve non-sectoral interests such as trade unions; black business and agriculture; and the presidency's advisory groups, consisting of the International Investment Advisory Council and made up of prominent CEOs of major international business corporations. The presidential special adviser also has a brief for economic affairs and for drafting technical plans for the implementation of NEPAD.

17 Dlamini-Zuma also had a strained relationship with her DG, Dr Olive Shisana, who then left her department for a more lucrative position with WHO. In addition, she took a firm stance against making public funds available for anti-retroviral drugs and, despite loud protests, made a year's community service obligatory for new medical school graduates.

18 Selebi's departure from the department was in keeping with his alleged peremptory and imperious nature. Two years into his five-year term, Pityana resigned as DG in January 2002. According to one report: 'Sources said differences had emerged between Pityana and Dlamini-Zuma and they had decided to part ways before these "reached boiling point"'. See *Business Day*, 10 January 2002, p. 1. At the time of writing, the deputy DG for Multilateral Affairs, Abdul Minty, was serving as Acting DG.

19 Pahad, Statement during the parliamentary debate on the budget of the Department of Foreign Affairs, Cape Town, 8 May 2001.

20 Dave Malcolmson, 'Foreign Policy Aligned at Heads of Mission Conference', *Global Dialogue*, vol. 5, no. 2, 2001, pp. 12–13.

21 Jacobs, 'Remaking the Presidency', p. 33.

22 See P. Nel, I. Taylor and J. van der Westhuizen, *South Africa's Multilateral Diplomacy and Global Change: The Limits of Reformism* (Aldershot: Ashgate Publishing Company, 2001), pp. 16–18; Hamill and Lee, 'A Middle Power Paradox?'.

23 See P. J. McGowan and F. Ahwireng-Obeng, 'Partner or Hegemon? South Africa in Africa', *Journal of Contemporary African Studies*, vol. 16, no. 2, 1998, pp. 165-95.

24 Interview with ex-Ambassador Barbara Masekela, Johannesburg, 17 February 2002.

25 Pahad, Statement during the parliamentary debate on the budget of the Department of Foreign Affairs, 8 May 2001.

26 Molly Cochran, 'A Pragmatist Perspective on Ethical Foreign Policy', in Karen E. Smith and Margot Light (eds), *Ethics and Foreign Policy* (Cambridge: Cambridge University Press, 2001), p. 68.

Chapter 3

1. Mark Malan, *SADC and Subregional Security*, ISS Monograph Series 19, February 1998, pp. 9–10.

2. The Freedom House criteria reflect Robert Dahl's institutional requirements for democratic states: elected representation, free and fair elections, political parties, inclusive of suffrage, the right to run for office, freedom of expression, associational autonomy, the rule of law and an efficient bureaucracy. See R. A. Dahl, Polyarchy: *Participation and Opposition* (New Haven, CT: Yale University Press, 1971). Freedom House adds civil and political liberties to this list.

3. Willie Breytenbach, 'Democracy in the SADC Region: A Comparative Overview', *African Security Review*, vol. 11, no. 4, 2002, p. 93.

4. *Ibid.*, p. 100.

5. Walter Tapfumaneyi, 'Regional Security Co-operation: A View from Zimbabwe', *Global Dialogue*, vol. 4, no. 2, August 1999, pp. 23, 25.

6. Concern was voiced at the SADC summit in August 1995 over the placement of security issues in the hands of one state – as was customary with other SADC sectoral approaches. Malan, *SADC and Subregional Security*, p. 13.

7. *Ibid.*, pp. 13-14. According to Denis Venter, the ISDSC was to become the Organ's secretariat. Venter, 'Regional Security in Sub-Saharan Africa', *African Insight*, vol. 26, no. 2, 1996, p. 173.

8. Horst Brammer, 'In Search of an Effective Regional Security Mechanism for Southern Africa', *Global Dialogue*, vol. 4, no. 2, August 1999, pp. 21–22.

9. Tapfumaneyi, 'Regional Security Co-operation', pp. 23, 25.

10. *Southscan*, vol. 16, no. 3, 9 February 2001, p. 5.

11. *Southscan, Monthly Review Bulletin*, September 2000, vol. 9, no. 9, p. 8.

12. Interview with Anthoni van Nieuwkerk, Johannesburg, 4 February 2002.

13. Paul Hare, *Angola's Last Best Chance for Peace: An Insider's Account of the Peace Process* (Washington DC: US Institute of Peace, 1998), p. 111.

14. South African Foreign Minister's address, South African Institute for International Affairs, Johannesburg, 1 November 1999.

15. Stephen Ellis and Tsepo Sechaba, *Comrades Against Apartheid: The ANC and the South African Communist Party in Exile* (London: James Currey, 1992), p. 101. The poor conditions in the camps and an unwillingness to defend the MPLA position eventually led to mutinies amongst disgruntled MK guerrillas in 1984.

16. See Alex Vines, 'Mercenaries, Human Rights and Legality', in Abdel-Fatau Musah and J. 'Kayode Fayemi (eds), Mercenaries: An African Security Dilemma (London: Pluto Press, 2000), p. 174.

17. *Southscan, Monthly Regional Bulletin*, February 2000, vol. 9, no. 2, p. 4.

18. *Ibid.*, p. 4.

19. Mandela claimed that, despite the fact that his government defended Kabila in a variety of international settings, Kabila ignored South African advice to make major reforms to the political system and put the Congo on the road to democracy. Independent Online, 19 January 2001, www.iol.co.za.

20. Jakkie Cilliers and Malan, *Peacekeeping in the DRC: MONUC and the Road to Peace*, ISS Monograph Series 66, October 2001, p. 47.

21. For example, Mbeki and the OAU head, Algerian President

Abdelaziz Bouteflika, sought to organise a 'Lusaka II' initiative in an effort to gain the compliance of all parties.

22 *Southscan, Monthly Review Bulletin*, August 2000, vol. 9, no. 8, p. 6.

23 *Southscan*, 23 February 2001, p. 5.

24 Cilliers and Malan, *Peacekeeping in the DRC*, p. 27.

25 Cited in Breytenbach, 'Failure of Security Co-operation in SADC', *South African Journal of International Affairs*, vol. 7, no. 1, 2000, p. 9.

26 Interview with Mbarouk N. Mbarouk, Tanzanian diplomat, London, 14 February 2001.

27 Costs were estimated at R5m; *Weekly Mail and Guardian*, 19 April 2002, www.mg.co.za.

28 International Crisis Group, 'Inter-Congolese Dialogue Process: Political Negotiation or Game of Bluff?', 16 November 2001, www.crisisweb.org/projects/repo rts; interview with Shannon Field, Institute for Global Dialogue, Pretoria, 17 February 2002; Institute for Global Dialogue, 'Potential Breaking Points in the ICD', report by the Institute for Global Dialogue for the Masire Facilitation Team, 15 February 2002.

29 *Independent Online* (Johannesburg), 19 April 2002, www.iol.co.za.

30 In addition to accusations that Joseph Kabila and the MLC's Jean-Pierre Bemba had come to an agreement on power-sharing in the transitional government in advance of the talks, there was considerable concern as to the compatibility of the two leaders and the ability of the RCD to scupper any arrangement. *Weekly Mail and Guardian*, 19 April 2002, www.mg.co.za.

31 Africa Institute, 'Report on the Africa Institute of SA Fact-Finding Mission to Zimbabwe', April 2001, p. 5.

32 The convening of an international donor conference in September 1998 seemed to offer a credible route to resolving Zimbabwe's land problem. Funding amounting to Z$7.4m was pledged to purchase 118 farms, but the inception phase never happened because of conditionalities on transparency of the process imposed by donors. However, within a year the cost to the Zimbabwean economy of sustaining the Congo operation had become apparent and, following the disclosure of irregularities in national accounting to underplay these costs, brought about a suspension of IMF loans of $193m and $140m.

33 John Makamure, chief economist, Zimbabwe Chamber of Commerce and Industry, 'New Finance Minister Gets Down to Serious Business', *Trader*, October 2000–January 2001, p. 22.

34 John Makumbe, 'South Africa's Quiet Diplomacy: Has It Worked?', paper delivered at a conference on the Zimbabwe crisis, South African Institute for International Affairs, Johannesburg, 14 February 2001.

35 See Kuseni Dlamini, Greg Mills and Neuma Grobbelaar, 'Rethink Quiet Diplomacy in Zimbabwe', *Mail and Guardian*, 9 May 2001. Such was the growing domestic sensitivity of the issue that Mbeki declared that critics of the government's 'quiet diplomacy' were racist. Mbeki, 'Clamour Over Zimbabwe Shows Continuing Racial Prejudice in SA', Sowetan, 26 March 2001.

36 *Independent Online* (Johannesburg), 25 February 2002, www.iol.co.za.

37 *Ibid.*, 19 July 2001 and 3 September 2001.

38 For a critical assessment of the NEPAD initiative, see Ian Taylor and Philip Nel, 'New Africa,

Globalisation and the Confines of Elite Reformism: Getting the Rhetoric Right, Getting the Strategy Wrong', *Third World Quarterly*, vol. 23, no. 1, 2002.

39 *The Sunday Independent* (Johannesburg), 17 February 2002.

40 *Independent Online*, 15 March 2002, www.iol.co.za.

41 *Daily Mail and Guardian*, 15 March 2002.

42 Jan van Eck, then with the Centre for Conflict Resolution in Cape Town, was an important source of advice and information.

43 Interview with Mbarouk, London, 14 February 2001; International Crisis Group, 'Burundi Peace Process: Tough Challenges Ahead', 27 August 2000, www.crisisweb.org/projects/reports.

44 These included a breakaway faction of the main Hutu party, the Conseil national pour la defense de la democratie (CNDD) and the Parti pour la liberation du peuple Hutu-Forces nationales de liberation. They directly threatened SANDF troops with violence if they took up their positions in Burundi.

45 International Crisis Group, 'One Hundred Days to Get the Peace Process Back on Track', 14 August 2001, www.crisisweb.org/projects/reports.

46 The International Crisis Group in particular has been highly critical of the Mandela mediation in terms of methodology as well as substance, characterising it as an agreement 'obtained by default and a forceps delivery'. International Crisis Group, 'Burundi: Neither Peace Nor War', ICG Africa Report 25, December 2000.

47 *SABC News*, 14 November 2001, www.sabcnews.com; interview with Richard Cornwell, Institute for Security Studies, Pretoria, 7 February 2002.

48 Interview with Gavin Cawthra, Defence Management Programme, Wits Business School, Johannesburg, 4 February 2002.

49 Interview with Eddy Moloka, Director, Africa Institute, Pretoria, 6 February 2002.

50 These instances where substantive measures have been utilised, such as the deployment of peacekeepers in Burundi or more recently a small contingent in the Congo, underscore the shallow capacity of the SANDF to sustain a mission of this kind.

Chapter 4

1 By one estimate, South Africa's destabilisation campaign cost the region $90bn between 1980 and 1988. See Kato Lambrechts, 'The SADC's Origins', in R. de Villiers and K. Lambrechts (eds), *The IGD Guide to the Southern African Development Community* (Johannesburg: Institute for Global Dialogue, 2001), p. 25.

2 See ANC, *Foreign Policy in a New Democratic South Africa* (ANC: Johannesburg, 1994).

3 O'Meara, O'Meara, 'Regional Economic Integration in Post-Apartheid South Africa', p. 233.

4 McGowan and Ahwireng-Obeng, 'Partner or Hegemon?', p. 166.

5 SACU consists of South Africa, Lesotho, Swaziland, Botswana and Namibia.

6 The portrait of under-development is indeed a grim one: 'In most southern African countries, more than half of the inhabitants live below the national poverty line; in some, most of the population do not have access to safe water and sanitation. This situation is compounded by the highly unequal income distribution throughout the region, with the richest 20% earning 50 and 60% of total income'. K. Lambrechts, 'The

SADC: A Developmental Profile', in de Villiers and Lambrechts (eds), *The IGD Guide to the Southern African Development Community*, p. 34.

7   A. Graumans, *SADC–EU Cooperation Beyond the Lomé Convention*, Occasional Paper 11 (Johannesburg: Foundation for Global Dialogue, 1997).

8   R. Davies, *South Africa in the SADC: Trade and Investment* (Cape Town: Centre for Southern African Studies, 1997).

9   World Bank, *Entering the 21st Century: World Investment Report 1999/2000* (Oxford: Oxford University Press, 2000), p. 271.

10   Interview with Faizal Ismail, director, Department of Trade and Industry, Pretoria, 6 February 2002.

11   Potential losses in customs revenue for some SADC countries such as Zambia (28%) and Zimbabwe (32%) are another source of concern. See Margaret Lee, 'SADC and the Creation of a Free Trade Area in Southern Africa', in Eddie Maloka (Ed) *A United States of Africa?* (Pretoria: Africa Institute of South Africa, 2001), p. 268. South African negotiators have also been accused of failure to consult with SADC or SADC partners during talks on the regional and international stage. Ibid, p. 260.

12   A. du Plessis, 'The Geopolitical Context: A Sea Change from Old to New Geopolitics', in Carlsnaes and Muller (eds), *Change and South African External Relations*, pp. 19–24.

13   The admission of the DRC into SADC has, by all accounts, been divisive. The DRC's war against internal adversaries and external aggressors has drawn SADC into the conflict, resulting in a rupture among its membership. There is a 'defence treaty bloc', led by Zimbabwe and made up of Angola, Namibia and the DRC; and, while not as cohesive, a 'peacemaking bloc', led by South Africa and made up of Tanzania, Mozambique and Botswana with implicit support from Zambia, Swaziland and Malawi. See R. Williams, 'Managing Regional Security', in de Villiers and Lambrechts (eds), *The IGD Guide to the Southern African Development Community*, pp. 115–17.

14   International Crisis Group, 'Zimbabwe's Election: The Stakes for Southern Africa', Harare/Brussels, 11 January 2002, www.crisisweb.org.

15   Matlosa, 'The Lesotho Conflict'.

16   S. Santho, 'Conflict Management and Post-Conflict Peace Building in Lesotho', in *Crisis in Lesotho*.

17   Statement on the African renaissance at Midrand and broadcast by the SA Broadcasting Corporation, 13 August 1998.

18   A. van Nieuwkerk, 'South Africa's Emerging Foreign Policy', in le Pere, van Nieuwkerk and Lambrechts (eds), *South Africa and Africa*, p. 45.

19   Department of Foreign Affairs, *A New African Initiative: Merger of the Millennium Africa Recovery Programme and Omega Plan*, 2001, www.dfa.gov.za/events/afrinit.htm.

20   The NAM was founded in the Yugoslav capital Belgrade in 1961. By 1998, it had 114 full members, as well as 30 observers. It is committed to principles of disarmament, the peaceful settlement of disputes, South–South cooperation, North–South dialogue and the reform of the UN Security Council. It has no permanent secretariat and has a rotating presidency that changes every three years. At its twelfth summit, South Africa was elected to the presidency. The OAU was formed in 1963 as a pan-African body with headquarters in Addis Ababa, Ethiopia. All independent

African states except Morocco are members. The G77 is a coalition of the world's poorer countries, formed in 1964 at the UNCTAD summit in Geneva, with the aim of collectively pressing for a major restructuring of the world economy. Originally, there were 77 members, but the group had grown to 124 by 1997. It remains a major forum for regular consultation among developing countries within the UN system.

[21] They are Algeria, Botswana, Cameroon, Egypt, Ethiopia, Gabon, Mali, Mauritius, Mozambique, Nigeria, Rwanda, Sao Tome and Principe, Senegal, South Africa and Tunisia.

[22] See 'NEPAD': A Historical Overview', February 2002, www.dfa.gov.za/docs/nepad2.htm

[23] See 'NEPAD' website for documents, outlooks and profiles:www.nepad.org

[24] Alex de Waal, 'What's new in the "New Partnership for Africa's Development"?', *International Affairs* 78:3 2002, page 466.

[25] OECD peer reviews are sectorally-based while those envisaged in NEPAD are much wider in scope as they include categories such as 'democracy and good political governance'. As of September 2003, 16 African countries had signed on to the APRM. See John Ohiorhenuan, 'NEPAD: thinking out of the box', paper presentation at the South African Institute for International Affairs, Johannesburg, 17 September 2003, page 14.

[26] In fact, net disbursements of aid fell from \$57bn in 2002 to \$46bn in 2003. William Shaw and Eung Y Kim, 'Living up to the Monterrey Commitments', Global Development Finance 2003, World Bank, Washington DC, 2003, www.worldbank.org/prospects/gdf2003>

[27] George Ayittey, Africa Unchained: the blueprint for development (Palgrave 2003).

[28] 'Africa: The Heart of the Matter', *The Economist*, 13–19 May 2000, p. 24.

[29] F. Kornegay, 'Beyond the OAU: African Union or Afro-Jamahiriya', *Global Dialogue*, vol. 5, no. 2, 2000, p. 3.

[30] According to one expert, 'Libya's efforts to circumvent the UN sanctions were behind Gaddafi's recent diplomatic rapproachment with sub-Saharan Africa'. Asteris Huliaris, 'Qadafi's Comeback: Libya and sub-Saharan Africa in the 1990s', *African Affairs* 2001, pg. 22

[31] M. Geneg, *Formation of the African Union, African Economic Community and Pan-African Parliament*, African Union and a Pan-African Parliament: Working Papers (Pretoria: Africa Institute Research Paper 63, 2000), p. 6.

[32] Statement at the Thirty-fifth Ordinary Session of the OAU Assembly of Heads of State and Government, Algiers, Algeria, 13 July 1999, www.anc.org.za/ancdocs/history/mbeki/1999/tm0713.html.

[33] Ibid. *African Affairs*

[34] Address by the chairperson of the Non-Aligned Movement, President Mbeki of South Africa, to the NAM Ministerial Meeting, UN, New York, 23 September 1999, www.anc.org.za/ancdocs/history/mbeki/1999/tm0923.html.

[35] P. Nel et al., 'Reformist Initiatives and South Africa's Multilateral Diplomacy: A Framework for Understanding', in Nel, Taylor and van der Westhuizen (eds), *South Africa's Multilateral Diplomacy*, pp. 2–3.

[36] Speech on the Occasion of the Consideration of the Budget Vote of the Presidency, National Assembly, 13 June 2000, www.anc.org.za/ancdocs/history/mbeki/2000/tm0613.html.

[37] I. Taylor, 'The "Mbeki Initiative"

and Reform of the Global Trade Regime', in Nel, Taylor and van der Westhuizen (eds), *South Africa's Multilateral Diplomacy*, p. 68.

38 Interview with Faisal Ishmael, Department of Trade and Industry, Pretoria, 6 February 2002.

39 Nel, Taylor and van der Westhuizen (eds), *South Africa's Multilateral Diplomacy*, constitutes the first analytical attempt to comprehensively examine the normative underpinnings, theoretical basis and empirical elements of South Africa's multilateral diplomacy. The thrust of the book is stated as to seek answers to the question: 'Is South Africa's multilateral diplomacy indeed contributing to global transformation, or is the effect of its initiatives rather that South Africa is contributing to the maintenance of a fundamentally flawed global order?' (p. 13).

40 *Ibid.*, p. 5.

41 G. le Pere and K. Lambrechts, 'Civil Society and Foreign Policy in South Africa', in J. van der Westhuizen (ed.), *Democratisation and Foreign Policy* (London: Pluto Press, 2002).

42 See, for example, J. Mathews, 'Power Shift', *Foreign Affairs*, vol. 76, no. 1, 1999.

43 See the cover of Newsweek magazine, 4 March 2002: 'Mbeki against the world: feuding with old comrades and AID activists, a lonely leader fights to save his presidency'.

44 G. le Pere and K. Lambrechts, 'Globalisation and National Identity Construction: Nation-building in South Africa', in S. Bekker and R. Prinsloo (eds), *Identity? Theory, Politics, History* (Pretoria: Human Sciences Research Council, 1999), pp. 24–32.

45 Van der Westhuizen, 'South Africa's Emergence as a Middle Power', p. 447. This accusation is countered by reference to South Africa's special characteristics. In the words of former (but now late) Foreign Minister Alfred Nzo, 'South Africa is a developing country with certain of the attributes of a developed, or industrialised country. This enables us to understand, and relate to, the concerns of both the south, as well as the north, and therefore to play a pivotal role in drawing them closer together to promote international development'. Remarks made during the Foreign Affairs Budget Vote, Cape Town: Senate, 16 May, 1996, cited in *ibid.*, p. 450.

46 J. van der Westhuizen, I. Taylor and P. Nel, 'Of Rogues, Rebels, Renegades and Reformers: South African Multilateralism in Context', in Nel, Taylor and van der Westhuizen (eds), *South Africa's Multilateral Diplomacy*, p. 122.

Conclusion

1 A. Stanger, 'Democratisation and the International System: The Foreign Policies of Interim Governments', in Y. Shain and J. Linz (eds), *Between States: Interim Government and Democratic Transitions* (Cambridge: Cambridge University Press, 1995), p. 255.

2 Adrian Guelke's point that the transition coincided with the loss of nearly 15,000 lives bears repeating. A. Guelke, *South Africa in Transition: The Misunderstood Miracle* (London: I. B. Taurus, 1999), p. 45.

3 Barber, *Jihad vs McWorld*, p. 4.

4 A. van Nieuwkerk, 'Implications for South Africa's Foreign Policy Beyond the Lesotho Crisis', *Accord Occasional Paper*, vol. 3, no. 99, pp. 1–4. Also see IISS, *Strategic Survey 2000–2001* (Oxford: Oxford

University Press for the IISS,
2001).

5 Lindy Heinecken, 'Facing a
Merciless Enemy: HIV/AIDS and
the South African Armed Forces',
Armed Forces and Society 29:2
2003, pg. 284